TROPICAL SHIPWRECKS

By Daniel &
Denise Berg

A VACATIONING DIVER'S GUIDE TO THE BAHAMAS AND CARIBBEAN

Library of Congress Catalog Card No. 89-084043
ISBN: 0-9616167-2-5

FOR ADDITIONAL COPIES, WRITE TO:
AQUA EXPLORERS, INC.
P.O. Box 116
East Rockaway, NY 11518

Copyright © 1989

ii

ABOUT THE AUTHORS

Dan Berg is a P.A.D.I. (Professional Association of Diving Instructors) Master Scuba Diver Trainer. He is a Specialty Instructor in Wreck Diving, Night Diving, Search and Recovery, Underwater Hunting, Deep Diving, Dry Suit Diving, U/W Metal Detector Hunting, U/W Archeology, and has written and teaches his own nationally approved Distinctive Specialties in Shipwreck Research, and U/W cinematography. Dan also holds certifications in Rescue and Environmental Marine Ecology. He is the Author of WRECK VALLEY, a record of shipwrecks off Long Island's South Shore, SHORE DIVER, a divers guide to Long Island's beach sites, publisher of the Wreck Valley Loran C Coordinate List, and co producer of the Wreck Valley Video Series, and Shipwrecks of Grand Cayman Video. His award winning underwater cinematography has been used on a variety of cable TV shows. Dan's photographs and articles have been printed in SKIN DIVER MAGAZINE, UNDERWATER USA, NAUTICAL BRASS, The FISHERMAN MAGAZINE plus many more.

Denise Berg is a P.A.D.I. certified open water diver with specialty ratings in Underwater Photography, Equipment Maintenance, and Shipwreck Research and is also a certified Regulator Repair Technician. Denise has done underwater modeling for nationally sold underwater videos. Denise and Dan have traveled extensively throughout the Caribbean in search of exciting new shipwrecks. Denise is also the co-owner of Aqua Explorers Inc. and Dive World Inc.

Dan and Denise have made many wreck diving excursions to locations such as Antiqua, Barbados, Bermuda, Bonaire, Cozumel, Curacao, Eleuthera, Florida, Grand Cayman, Grenada, Jamaica, Kaui, Maui, New Jersey, North Carolina, Paradise Island, Pennsylvania, Puerto Rico, Saint Croix, Saint Lucia, Saint Thomas and Tortola. Avid wreck divers of the Caribbean seas, Dan and Dee became aware of the need for a complete text on Caribbean shipwrecks. When they could find no historical information on any of the wrecks they had visited, they decided that it was time to publish information and provide photographs on as many wrecks as possible. They talked with many of the top Caribbean wreck divers and combined this information with extensive research and photographs, which we all know are worth a thousand words, into a complete easily indexed reference manual. The result of their work will enable all vacationing divers to be knowledgeable about the wrecks they are diving.

ACKNOWLEDGEMENTS

We would like to thank the following for their time, knowledge and information. Christine Berg for editing and proof reading; our good friend Captain Steve Bielenda for his advice and support; James Abbot, Glenroy Adams, Jimmy Antoine, Ellswoth Boyd, Laura F. Brown, Al Catalfumo, Chip Cooper, Dennis Reeves Cooper, George Condiff, Stuart Cove, Cathy Cush, Chris Dillon, Barbara Doernbach, Joe Donahue, Rudolph Dunken, Tony Felgate, Carl Fismer, Lou Flotte, Al Forns, Steve Frink, Hank Garvin, Charlet Green, Willie Hassel, Aaron Hirsh, Bill Holtgren, Ann C. House, Keath Ipson, Hank Keats, Mary Ellen Kenny, Elizabeth Koch, Joe Koppelman, Mason Logie, Maureen Morgenthien, Andre Nahr, Gabrielle Nahr, Keith Nichols, Frazier Nivens, Jeffrey Parrish, Ray Post, Kenneth Samuel, Jim Scheiner, Jerry Schnabel, Rick Schwarz, Nancy Sefton, Herb Segars, Joel Senna, William Schell, Steve Simonsen, Jorma J. Sjoblom, Robert Stephens, Suzie Swygert, Debbie Powers Vogel, Joe Vogel, Julie Wang, Chloe Zimmerman; our diving partners Rick Schwarz, Steve Jonassen and Bill Campbell; last, but certainly not least, Winfred Berg, Donald Berg and Dennis Berg for all of their time, energy, and technical advice.

UNDERWATER PHOTOGRAPHY

We would like to acknowledge and sincerely thank all who have donated their beautiful underwater photographs for this book. It is these unselfish professionals who made this publication possible, In alphabetical order they are; Glenroy Adams, Al Catalfumo, Chip Cooper, Cathy Cush, Tony Felgate, Carl Fismer, Stephen Frink, Lucien Flotte, Al Forns, Keith Ipson, Hank Keats, Joe Koppelman, J.C. Laurier, Mason Logie, Gary Moore, Andre Nahr, Frazier Nivens, Jeffrey Parrish, Doug Perrine, Courtney Platt, James B. Scheiner, Nancy Sefton, Herb Segars, Steve Simonsen, Robert "Desi" Stephens and our old friends Ed Tiedemann and Jeanne Tiedemann.

HOW TO USE

This text was designed to be a diver's guide to shipwrecks located in the Caribbean and Bahamas. It can be used in any number of ways. Divers who are going to an island on vacation can reference this manual to find the best wrecks to dive on, or it can be used to help decide on a destination for your vacation. This book can also aid in dive planning. Each site contains pertinent information such as the wreck's depth, currents, visibility, and types of aquatic life. You will also find many photos, both topside and underwater. Historical information in this guide will help you to have a better understanding of each wreck. The destinations are in alphabetical order, first by area, then by island, and finally by the wreck's name. You can look up an area, island, or wreck which are all indexed in the back of the book. Note that some wrecks are known by two, three, or even four different names. Some of these names were given to unknown wrecks, some are nicknames, and some are the vessel's original name which had been changed before the ship's sinking.

We have covered all wrecks that we have knowledge of and make no claims that this text is a complete listing of all Caribbean ship wrecks. Each year old wrecks are discovered, and new ones are sunk. If you have any information on a shipwreck located in the Caribbean or Bahamas that is presently being enjoyed by sport divers, please contact the publisher. We will be more then happy to update the text for future printings.

The easiest way to look up a particular wreck within this reference manual is to look up the name you have for the wreck in the index, which is found in the back of the book. We've tried to index all known names of each wreck for easy reference.

WRECK DIVING

Each year thousands of people become certified scuba divers all over the world. These people have different goals in mind upon reaching their first training certification level. Some want to dive locally all year round in good or poor visibility, some may only plan on warm weather diving, and others may simply become certified so they can dive on their vacations to the beautiful clear Caribbean sea. However, there are a large number of divers who have channeled their time and energy into the fascinating world of shipwrecks.

Wreck diving is thrilling for many reasons. Foremost, the thought of finding sunken treasure would be exciting to anyone. More realistically, treasures are rarely found, but wreck dives are like a short visit into history. To explore the nostalgic value of each ship is to realize that the vessel was once built with a specific goal in mind; perhaps it was designed as a warship, cargo vessel, freighter or a luxury liner with a crew who once lived on board doing the normal things of everyday life. Unfortunately the ship and crew may have suffered a great tragedy. Of course, any sinking that involved lost lives was a disaster incomparable to any other.

There is no dive experience equal to that of slowly descending into the quiet sea with only the noise of bubbles around you and then suddenly seeing a large vessel sitting alone in the sand, seemingly inviting all divers to explore its remains. To observe or photograph the wreck, an artifact or the large amount of marine life that thrives on and around each wreck is something that a wreck diver will remember forever.

Contrary to most beliefs, wreck diving is not only for the most experienced diver. Many ships are in water shallow enough for all divers to enjoy, and an exciting experience on a wreck does not have to mean penetration. A lot of the wrecks are broken up into huge debris fields scattered over the ocean floor. Others were sunk intentionally with large holes cut through their steel plating, allowing for plenty of ambient light to filter through much of the interior. Wreck penetration of a shipwreck should only be done by experienced divers with the proper training and equipment. We feel that if good common sense is followed, all divers can enjoy exploring these fascinating time capsules into history.

AREA INDEX

BAHAMAS

THE BAHAMAS

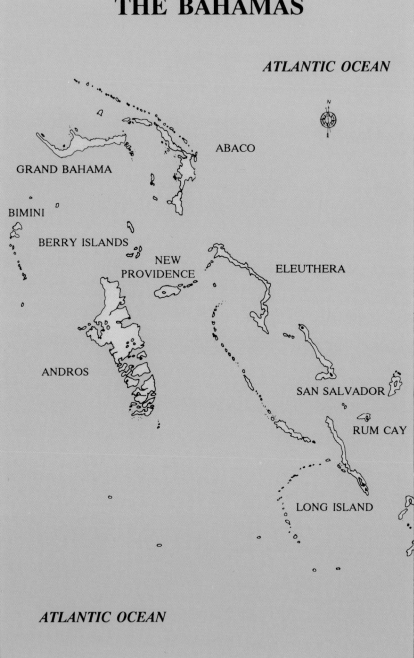

ATLANTIC OCEAN

ABACO

GRAND BAHAMA

BIMINI

BERRY ISLANDS

NEW PROVIDENCE

ELEUTHERA

ANDROS

SAN SALVADOR

RUM CAY

LONG ISLAND

ATLANTIC OCEAN

ABACO

The Abacos islands are located in the northeast section of the Bahamas approximately 170 miles from Miami, Florida. The two largest islands are Great Abaco and Little Abaco.

The best diving off Abaco is between its eastern shores and cays that are protected from the Atlantic Ocean by barrier reefs. Green Turtle Cay, Treasure Cay and Man of War Cay all offer excellent diving. Diving Abaco centers around a reef that is one of the longest in the world, measuring about 150 miles.

U.S.S. ADIRONDACK

The *U.S.S. Adirondack* was an Ossipee class wooden screw sloop built in 1861 at the New York Navy Yard. She was launched on February 22, 1862, and commissioned in June of the same year. This union gun boat was 207 feet long, had a 38 foot beam, weighed 1,240 gross tons, and was powered by both sail and steam. The *Adirondack* was part of the South Atlantic Blockading Squadron. On August 23, 1862, while on a voyage from Port Royal to Nassau, she ran aground on Little Bahama Bank. Her crew was rescued by the vessel *Canadaigua*, but all salvage attempts of the ship failed. The *Adirondack* broke up in the surf and sunk.

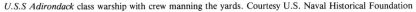

U.S.S Adirondack class warship with crew manning the yards. Courtesy U.S. Naval Historical Foundation

The scattered remains of this warship rest in 10 to 30 feet of water. Divers can still see two of her 11 inch bore cannons that are about twelve feet long and weigh about 10,000 pounds each. Twelve smaller cannons can also be sighted while exploring the wreckage.

BARGE

The *Barge* wreck is the remains of a World War II landing craft. She rests in a small channel off Fiddle Key, in 40 feet of water and is badly deteriorated. The wreck has broken apart and scattered over a large area but remains to be an absolutely fantastic site for macro photography.

BONITA

The *Bonita*, also known as *Bonvita*, was once utilized by the British to evacuate soldiers from Dunkirk and was later used as a houseboat. Brendal, the owner of Brendal's Dive shop, purchased the vessel in order to sink her as a dive site and fish haven. She now rests in 60 feet of water and is used as a feeding station for groupers.

DEMIRA

Originally built in the Bahamas, the *Demira* was a 411 foot long, steel hulled sailing freighter. She was sunk by damage incurred from a hurricane in 1928.

The *Demira* has become a nice shallow water dive. Sitting in only 30 feet of water, she allows divers plenty of bottom time to fully explore her wreckage.

U.S.S. SAN JACINTO

This warship is yet another civil war gunboat. The *U.S.S. San Jacinto* was one of the earliest American built steam vessels. In fact, she was built as an experimental ship to test the technology of new propulsion concepts. She was laid down by the New York Navy Yard in August of 1847 and launched on April 16, 1850. A screw frigate, the *Jacinto* was 234 feet long, and had a 38 foot beam. During her life on the sea she was plagued by unreliable machinery which was always in need of repair.

After years of her valuable and interesting service, which included providing

Bow of the *U.S.S. San Jacinto*. Drawing courtesy U.S. Naval Historical Center.

U.S.S. San Jacinto. Courtesy Steamship Historical Society Collection, University of Baltimore Library.

naval support to northern troops, capturing the blockade runners *Lizzie Davis, Fox, Edward, Roebuck* and *Lealtad*; diplomatic missions overseas; and involvement in China's Second Opium War, the *San Jacinto* met her doom by running aground on New Year's Day, 1865. At the time of her demise, she was engaged in blockade duty for the U.S. Navy. Her guns and some of her provisions were recovered, but all efforts to salvage the vessel were unsuccessful.

This wreck sits on a slope with a maximum depth of 40 feet. Her structure is scattered due to the constant pounding of the sea which leaves us no clue as to the shape she once held. On our visit we encountered a large friendly green moray eel (Gymnothorax Funebris). To say the least, he was eager for a free handout, and became a very willing model.

SAN JUAN EVANGELISTA

The Spanish Galleon *San Juan Evangelista* was part of the Armada de Barlovento of Spain.

In the year 1714, she was en route from Veracruz to Puerto Rico, transporting a military payroll of 300,000 pesos, when a violent storm forced her aground. The ship was left resting high and dry on a reef which made for easy salvage operations. Her treasure and her cannons were recovered.

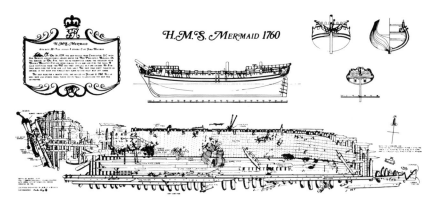

The *H.M.S. Mermaid* in her present condition on the ocean floor. Courtesy Carl Fismer, Spanish Main Treasure Company.

H.M.S. MERMAID

The *H.M.S. Mermaid*, an English warship under the command of Captain James Hackman, set sail from Charleston, South Carolina to New Providence on December 1, 1759. On the morning of December 4th, the ship was blown into the breakers by gail force winds blowing from the northeast which forced her to anchor. The *Mermaid* had tried to anchor three times, but on each attempt the force of the storm snapped her line, driving her closer to a shallow reef. At 8:00 AM Captain Hackman, in an attempt to lighten his vessel with the hopes of allowing her to pass over the reef, ordered her guns to be cast overboard. This attempt only prolonged the inevitable fate. The *Mermaid* finally ran aground a half mile from shore. For a month the vessel's hull stood up to the ocean's pounding, allowing time for all of her stores to be salvaged. On January 6, 1760, the *Mermaid* finally collapsed and sunk beneath the waves.

The location of this site remained unknown until 1987 when the Spanish Main Treasure Company with the use of a proton magnetometer was able to find her resting spot. According to Carl Fismer, a noted treasure hunter, the site was found after locating one of her anchors in about 40 feet of water. This clue lead the team to a second anchor, a third, and then a fourth. Each anchor brought the treasure hunters closer to the *H.M.S. Mermaid*. They found her cannons in 30 feet of water, and finally the remains of her hull were found in only ten feet.

The Spanish Main Treasure Company preserved the historical integrity of the site. Duke Long, the company's cartographer, drew up detailed drawings of the wreckage. Although this site was never thought to contain treasure, the group did recover some very interesting artifacts including two complete

5

Cannon from the *H.M.S. Mermaid.*
Photo courtesy Carl Fismer, Spanish
Main Treasure Company.

Diver surveying the *Mermaid* wreck. Photo courtesy Carl Fismer.

cooking hearths, which are the first intact ones ever to be salvaged.

Today, the wreck can be found off Mermaid Beach and explored by sport divers and snorkelers. Walkers Cay Diving runs trips to the wreck regularly, and who knows what a lucky diver might find.

TRAIN WRECK

The *Train Wreck* is not one, but two steam locomotive wrecks. We have not found any historical information, but they were most likely being transported on a barge when struck by some bad weather.

This site is sitting in only ten feet of water, and is excellent for snorkeling. The wreckage is scattered, so don't expect to see two complete trains sitting on the bottom. While exploring the wreckage, divers are able to see the locomotive's wheels, ballast pile, boilers, and engines.

This area is covered with fire coral, so be careful not to touch anything unless you're sure of what it is. Wearing gloves for protection is also a good idea.

Barbara Doerenbach explores the *Train Wreck* near Abaco. Photo by Stephen Frink.

ANDROS

Andros is the largest group of cays and islands, but least populated or explored of the Bahamas. Located 170 miles southeast of Miami, much of the island is covered with palm trees and tropical forests. Most tourist accommodations are found on North Andros, but don't expact too much in the way of night life.

Off the east coast of Andros lie 140 miles of barrier reef. The reef always offers excellent visibility, averaging 100 feet, and most dives are done between 25 and 70 feet. More experienced divers can go outside the reef where wall dives and drift dives border the 6,000 foot deep trench of the "Tongue of the Ocean". When divers are looking for something to do during surface intervals, they should try their hand at bonefishing since Andros is known as the bonefishing capital of the world.

LCM BARGE

The *LCM* wreck or *Barge Wreck*, as she is more commonly called, was a World War II landing craft. She was used to transport military troops onto the beach where her drop front door would open and allow the amphibious troops to walk, run, or crawl out.

In February of 1963, a local dive operator sunk the *LCM* in order to attract fish, and create a site for divers. The *LCM* has managed to do both magnificently. This long, rectangular shaped wreck sits upright in 70 feet of water. Her wheel house is in the stern where divers can still photograph her wheel. The wreck is home to a wide assortment of marine life which include a tame grouper. Fish feeding has become very popular on this site.

MARIAN

The *Marian* was a barge that apparently flipped over in 1987. The barge is fairly large, measuring about 100 feet long with a 40 foot beam. She sits in 70 feet of water. The Navy tried to raise the barge, but for some unknown reason its attempts failed. Near this site are also the remains of a crane that was used in the salvage attempt.

This wreck has already attracted some fish. In another year or two, when coral and sponge start to cover her, she should make for a great little fish haven.

POTOMAC

The *Potomac* was a British, steel hulled tanker built in 1893 by A & J Inglis Co. and owned by the Anglo American Oil Co. She was 345.2 feet long, 44.2 feet wide, weighed 3,858 gross tons, and had 426 nph triple expansion engines.

On September 26, 1929, while on a voyage from Baytown to London and Hull, the *Potomac* was caught in a hurricane and ran aground on the north end of Andros. The big ship was then broken in half by the relentless pounding of the sea.

The *Potomac* wreck lies scattered in only 18 to 20 feet of water. Divers can still distinguish her bow section, which remains upright, and her boilers from the rest of the wreck. Other parts of the wreck can still be seen breaking the surface.

Wreck of the *Potomac* near Andros, Bahamas. Photo by Stephen Frink.

BERRY ISLANDS

The Berry Islands are comprised of over thirty small islands with the largest and most frequented by tourists being Great Harbour Cay and Chub Cay. The Berry Islands lie 35 miles north of Nassau, and are known for their excellent game fishing, bonefishing, and of course diving. There are miles of wall diving to be done along the barrier reef of Chub Cay. Due to the great visibility, averaging over 100 feet, and the large assortment of marine life living on the reef, divers will find many nice photo opportunities.

PANTHER

The *Panther* wreck was a steel, 70 foot long tug boat. She rests on a slight starboard tilt in 60 feet of water still completely intact and upright. The cause and actual date of her sinking is still unknown.

Wide angle photography is best for this dive. Dramatic bow or stern shots, or photos taken of divers entering her wheel house should result in unique photos worth framing. The *Panther* is, to say the least, a beautiful picture perfect shipwreck.

Port side of the *Panther*, a 70 foot long tugboat sitting in 60 feet of water. Photo courtesy Cathie Cush.

PLANE WRECK

This site is a bit more than just a four seated, single engine *Piper* airplane. Other wreckage close by includes a *Toyota* truck and a *Ford* van. In our opinion, this site should be called *"The Junkyard"*. Depth of the assorted wreckage ranges from 40 to 60 feet, and the plane, van and truck are all decent photo opportunities.

BIMINI

A group of islands known as Bimini lie about 50 miles from Miami and 105 miles from Nassau. The two main islands are North Bimini and South Bimini. The waters off Bimini are known as the "Big Game Fishing Capital of the World". They also offer excellent panfishing and bonefishing.

Due to the small size of the islands, all dive sights can be reached quickly by boat. The best wall dives are off the west coast of Bimini, while the barrier reefs that surround the island are enriched with black coral gardens, beautiful sponges and blue holes.

SAPONA

The *Sapona*, which was a ferro-concrete steamer is also known as the *Concrete Wreck*. She was a 350 foot concrete hulled freighter, designed by Henry Ford and built in 1919 by Liberty Ship Building Co. in Brunswick, Ga. This 2,795 ton vessel was originally christened the *Lone Star*. She was one of a handful of ships built with steel reinforced concrete. This type of construction was done in an effort to conserve on precious steel during World War I.

Due to the extreme weight of this vessel, the *Lone Star* quickly proved that she was not cost efficient to operate and was sold soon after. A few years later, the *Lone Star*, which was by this time renamed *Sapona*, was purchased by a Bahamian who used the vessel to store prohibition whiskey. Rum runners would cruise to and from Florida picking up their illegal cargo from the *Sapona*, which was moored just offshore of Bimini.

In 1926, a severe hurricane hit Bimini. Even though the *Sapona* had been moved to a safe protected area, she was broken into two after being bounced off of the sea bed by massive merciless waves.

During World War II, the *Sapona* was utilized once again, this time as a

The rusting hulk of the *Sapona* resting in only 15 to 20 feet of water. Photo courtesy Cathie Cush.

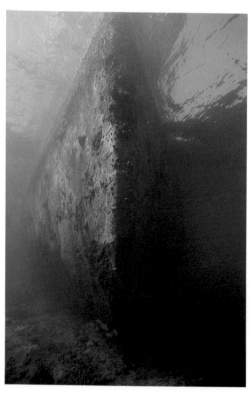

Coral encrusted bow, resting on a hard sea bed. Photo courtesy Jozef Koppelman.

Light filters into much of the *Sapona's* interior. Photo by Jozef Koppelman.

Four bladed steel propeller. Photo
courtesy Jozef Koppelman.

target for bombing practice. Air Force and Navy planes flew from Florida to Bimini to drop bombs on the *Sapona*. Accuracy of their staffing runs were improved by firing 30 caliber bullets into her rusting hulk.

Today, the wreck of the *Sapona* rests in only 15 to 20 feet of water. She is seen by some as an ugly, rusting hulk sticking out of an otherwise empty sea, and by others as a wonderful underwater sanctuary for all types of marine creatures. Due to her depth, this site can be explored by snorkelers as well as scuba divers. Visitors of the *Sapona* will see yellow tails, blue tangs, pufferfish, stingrays, queen and french angelfish, barracudas, and jacks. Just be careful of the fire coral which abounds on this wreck.

ELEUTHERA

Eleuthera is a long, narrow island with a population of 9,000. Most Eleuthera diving is offered around Spanish Wells, Harbour Islands, and North Eleuthera. Aside from the wrecks we've listed to dive on, there are many other interesting dive sites to visit. One of the most unique spots is called Current Cut. Current Cut is between Eleuthera and the smaller channel island where a 100 yard channel connects Eleuthera Sound with the ocean. Tide changes cause millions of gallons of water to pass through the channel at speeds of up to ten knots. Divers usually make two or three passes lasting from ten to 12 minutes each. This vivacious current is stronger than the divers, and more often than not sends them flying and tumbling. It is best to wear a wet suit for protection at this site to avoid cuts from coral, while relaxing and riding the current.

ARIMOROA

This 260 foot Lebanese freighter is also known as the *Freighter Wreck*, or the *Egg Island Wreck*. While en route from South America to Europe, this steel hulled vessel was run purposely aground in May of 1970. It is not known why, but a fire started in her galley, and spread with such speed and fury that her captain decided to save the crew by heading at full steam toward the nearest visible land, Egg Island. At the time of this unfortunate accident, the *Arimoroa* was carrying a cargo of guano-based fertilizer. All of her crew made it to land without injury.

The fire continued smoldering for almost three months. During this time sea water flushed her high-phosphate cargo out through the ship's cracked keel. For a few years afterwards, the surrounding area became barren as the high phosphate levels poisoned the reef's normal variety of sea life.

Diver swims around stern of the *Arimoroa*.
Photo courtesy Robert "Desi" Stephens.

Drawing of the *Arimoroa*. Courtesy Steve Bielenda collection.

Fortunately this would soon change.

Today, the badly burnt rusting remains of the *Arimoroa* sit perfectly upright in 25 feet of water on a hard limestone bottom. From a distance the *Arimoroa* looks like a ship at anchor, but on closer inspection it is easy to see that she will never sail again. All around the main wreckage is a debris field composed of steel hull plates, deck winches and various other machinery.

One of the most intriguing aspects of this wreck is the impressive amount of fish that now congregate around her hull. Desi Stephens, a local dive operator, reports seeing schools of 50 to 100 gray angels, an amount that is extremely unusual for this species. Other inhabitants include dozens of yellow stingrays, snappers, groupers and huge parrot fish. This drastic turn around of aquatic life has been studied by scientists from the University of Miami, the Rosenstiel School and the Florida Institute of Technology. They have so far counted over 60 species of fish. Some specialists say that it's due to the organic qualities of her fertilizer cargo, but whatever the reason, the fish seen on this site will certainly impress even the most seasoned Caribbean diver.

CARNARVON

The *Carnarvon* was a 186 foot long, steel hulled Welsh freighter. This vessel ran aground off of North Eleuthera back in 1916. She sits on a sand bottom in shallow water of only 25 to 35 feet which makes it possible for long relaxing dives. Her huge anchors, propeller, boilers and engines are good photo opportunities.

Diver explores wreckage of the *Cienfuegos*. Photo by Jeffrey Parrish.

CIENFUEGOS

The *Cienfuegos* was a Ward Line passenger liner. An American steam-ship, she was launched from the John Roach & Sons Shipyard in Chester, Pennsylvania in 1883. She was 292 feet in length, 39 feet 8 inches in breadth, had a draught of 22 feet, and weighed 2,332 tons. Her iron hull was divided into six watertight compartments.

On February 5, 1895, while under the command of Captain B.F. Hoyt Jr., the *Cienfuegos* ran aground on a shallow coral reef. According to the original New York Times article, "the vessel struck a reef while the seas were calm." Days later, one of the members of the *Cienfuegos* crew gave a slightly different account; "On the morning of Feb. 4 about 4:30 o'clock, during a strong northwest gale, while enormous seas were running and weather was hazy, the steamer ran on a reef or small coral islet, about five miles north of Harbor Island and forty-five miles from Nassau." Fortunately, all passengers and crew survived, all very thankful for the skill of the native seamen who were ferrying all to shore. One life boat with women and children aboard capsized, but two natives instantly plunged into the water and recovered all passengers before anyone drowned.

The *Cienfuegos* wreck now lies off the north tip of North Eleuthera and is scattered in ten to 35 feet of water. Most of her remains lie very flat which makes this wreck a testament to the merciless strength and power of the sea. Divers will find her bow sitting against a reef, her steam powered engine and boilers still recognizable.

A short distance away from the *Cienfuegos* lies the *Train Wreck*.

MAN OF WAR

The *Man Of War* wreck is the remains of two unknown vessels. The first is said by many researchers to be one of Columbus's ships. She sits on top of a coral reef only 200 yards east of the *Cienfuegos* wreck. The only thing still visible at this site is a big pile of ballast stones.

Depth at the site ranges from five to 30 feet, and visibility is usually excellent.

The second wreck is a steel vessel, approximately 120 feet long. Her propeller, engine, and some small pieces of brass are scattered outside the reef.

TRAIN WRECK

Wheel trucks from the *Train Wreck* suck in 1865. Photo by Jeffrey Parrish.

Although this is not a shipwreck in the true sense of the word, this is the remains of a barge that was carrying a steam locomotive. In 1865, the barge was caught in a violent storm and smashed onto an area referred to as Devil's Backbone located off of North Eleuthera.

The wreck which rests in 15 to 25 feet of water is very interesting because almost all traces of the barge have been either buried or eaten by Teredos (wood eating worms). All that remains to be seen are wheels, wheel trucks, a boiler plate assembly from the *Train*, and many brass spikes, coal, and ballast stone which originated from the barge.

Visibility on an average day ranges from 40 to 80 feet, and on occasion can be as good as 80 to 100 feet.

GRAND BAHAMA

Grand Bahama is conveniently located 60 miles from the Florida coast and is the fourth largest island in the Bahamas. The island is about 90 miles long and ranges in width from two to eight miles. The Underwater Explorers Society (UNEXSO) which is based in Lucaya is a great attraction for divers as well as non divers. Besides being a full service dive facility, there is a library and the Museum of Diving History.

Marine life abounds in the waters of Grand Bahama, and night diving is quite popular here. There are a large variety of coral reefs, walls, blue holes, caves, and of course wrecks.

JOSE

This steel hulled workboat named *Jose* is also known as the *Joise*. The vessel had been abandoned and left tied to a bulkhead behind a closed hotel. When the hotel was renovated in order to be reopened, the owners called Ollie Ferguson, a dive master at UNEXSO, (Underwater Explorers Society) to get rid of the vessel. She was 45 feet long by 20 feet wide and had once been used as a dive boat for an English commercial diving company.

On June 19, 1986, UNEXSO towed the vessel from her mooring in the Lucayan Marina to her present location. With the help of their crew consisting of Warren Manning, Glen Terquest, Steve Watson and Ollie Ferguson, UNEXSO pumped water into her hull until she was completely full. It took only 22 seconds for the *Jose* to reach the ocean floor. The *Jose* is now an artificial reef, and sits upright and intact on a slight starboard tilt in 65 feet of water. This is an excellent beginner wreck drive.

SUGAR WRECK

This unidentified shipwreck lies in about 15 to 20 feet of water, north of Memory Rock. She is totally out of sight from land, so local dive operators must rely on Loran in order to locate the wreck. The wreckage of this ship is scattered but mostly clustered into three main piles of debris on a sand bottom.

Thought by many to be a sunken barge, this steel wreck is home to some large great barracuda (Sphyraena Barracuda) ranging from four to six feet in length.

THEO'S WRECK

Originally named the *M.V. Logna*, this ship was built in Norway in 1954 as a cargo vessel. She was 228 feet long and had a 35 foot beam. In 1969 she was purchased by the Bahama Cement Company, and her name was changed to *M/V Island Cement*. She was then used to transport gravel and cement. In 1981, the vessel was on her last legs and ready to be scrapped.

Stern of *Theo's Wreck,* sunk in 1982. Courtesy UNEXSO.

Fortunately for the diving community, Theopolis Galanoupoulos, who was an engineer working for the cement company, came up with the idea of creating an artificial reef for all to enjoy instead of scrapping the vessel.

In 1982, after extensive preparations which included cutting large holes in her deck and hull to allow divers to safely explore the ship's interior, the vessel was taken out of port and sunk off Silver Beach Inlet, Grand Bahama Island. The sinking, which was a joint effort of UNEXSO and the Bahama Cement Co., took only four hours.

Today, *Theo's Wreck*, which has been once again renamed after the engineer who thought of sinking her, rests on her port side in 95 to 110 feet of water. The wreck is massive, completely intact and very photogenic. Her stern is actually perched on the edge of the famous Grand Bahama Ledge, where the continental shelf drops abruptly to a depth of 5000 feet. There is easy access into her pilot house and her cargo hold. Wide angle photographs or video of her bow or stern will definitely be the highlight of any wreck diver's vacation to Freeport.

LONG ISLAND

Long Island is located 160 miles southeast of Nassau and has a population of about 3,500. The island is 60 feet long by about 1.5 miles wide. Most activities on Long Island are operated by the Stella Maris Inn and Estate.

Diving arrangements are easily made on Long Island. One of the more popular dives is a site called Shark Reef which is often visited by Stella Maris dive boats. Divers can witness shark feeding done by the divemasters in about 35 feet of water. As you can imagine, this makes quite an exciting photo opportunity.

MV COMBERBACH

The *MV Comberbach* was a 103 foot, British, steel hulled freighter built in 1948. She was last operated by the Stella Maris Inn from 1980 through 1986 and then sunk in the summer of 1986 to form an artificial reef off Cape Santa Maria. She now rests in 100 feet of water off the west side of Long Island.

The vessel had been prepared for safe diver exploration prior to her sinking. For example, all of her compartments were opened allowing for easy and safe wreck penetration. There are usually no currents at the site, and water clarity is excellent.

Bow of the *Comberbach*. Courtesy Stella Maris Diving.

The *Comberbach* is sitting upright and intact. Some marine growth has already developed on her structure. Visibility at a norm is exceptionally good, so photographers naturally visit the site often. According to veteran diver Joerg Friese, there is a family of six very tame Nassau Groupers living on the wreck. Joerg goes on to say that the top of the wreck, the roof, smoke stack, etc. is in 65 feet of water, and inside her cargo hold is a 1975 Ford, which was formerly a Bell Telephone utility van.

Nearby are the remains of a 45 foot pleasure craft. Stella Maris Diving is also planning to sink another vessel on this site plus an aircraft.

NO NAME WRECK

This unidentified shipwreck is known as the *No Name Wreck*. The name was originated by photo journalist Stephen Frink. Steve had photographed, and written an article on the area referring to the site as "*No Name Wreck*", and since then the name has stuck.

This wreck is assumed by some to be the *H.M.S. Southhampton*. The *Southhampton* was a 32 gun English Frigate that wrecked on a reef under the command on Captain Sir James Lucas Yeo on November 27, 1812. The wreck was located when spotted from an airplane being flown by Stella Maris Diving. It was first dove back in 1970 and appears to be from the

Scattered remains of the *No Name Wreck*. Courtesy Elizabeth Koch, Stella Maris Diving.

early 1800's.

The wreck is flattened and scattered out except for her boilers, engine frame, piston, and crank shaft which can still be recognized. The *No Name Wreck* stretches out over a huge area of some 300 feet in width, and almost 800 feet in length. On the site are four anchors, three propellers, and a pile of anchor chain.

Since the location is exposed to the prevailing winds it should only be dove in good weather. It is also a good site for beginner divers as well as snorkelers.

NEW PROVIDENCE

New Providence is located in the center of the Bahama islands, and has a population of about 140,000. The popular vacation spot of Paradise Island is connected to New Providence by a bridge. The island offers everything for tourists that want to be busy day and night. There are many discos, luxury hotels, casinos, cruise ships and excellent restaurants.

There is a large choice of dive sites off of New Providence that begin at ten feet. They range from reefs to underwater movie props left behind by

23

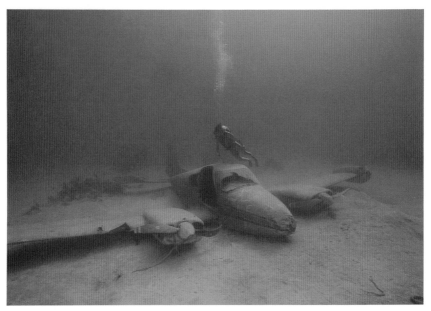

Cessna aircraft used as a prop in the Jaws 3 movie. Photo by Keith Ipson.

movie producers, all of which are surrounded with beautiful Caribbean scenery.

AIRPLANE

This Airplane wreck was a small *Cessna 310* that was originally used as a prop in the Jaws 3 movie. The *Cessna* Aircraft Company was founded in December 1927 by Clyde V Cessna. Modern day *Cessna* airplanes are popular light crafts purchased for business as well as private use.

According to Ray Post, a local dive operator, the aircraft was purposely crashed into the sea by a stunt pilot then raised and re-sunk in her present location. She is now sitting close to Clifton Wall in 50 feet of water.

ALCORA

The *Alcora* was a drug smuggling freighter, 130 feet in length. She was confiscated by the Bahamian government and sunk by local dive operators in 1983. She now rests on a sand bottom off Rose Island in 80 feet of water, upright and intact. Divers can swim through her two cargo holds, her engine room or just enjoy exploring the exterior of the wreck. Visibility on the wreck is usually good, but it can at times be a little hazy.

ANTINQUE

B-25 bomber. Photo courtesy National Archives.

LCT landing craft. This wreck was used in a fight scene in the James Bond Thunderball Movie. Photo courtesy National Archives.

The *Antinque* wreck was another drug smuggler, 40 feet in length. She had been confiscated by the government and was building up a very heavy dockage bill when a local resident decided that he wanted the boat. After paying the dockage fee, he pulled her into the harbor where she sank on him. She was later raised and re-sunk 200 yards west of the *Tears Of Allah* wreck.

B-25

The *B-25* wreck was a war plane that crashed into the sea during the Second World War. Most of the wreckage which is on the north side of Golden Key has become scattered and flattened out. Some parts of the Bomber can still be recognized including her wheels, landing gear, and engine. The plane rests on a sandy bottom in 20 to 30 feet of water.

LCT WRECK

The *LCT* wreck is a landing craft from the Second World War. This site is also known as *LST* or *Thunderball*. The wreck was used in a fight scene in the James Bond, Thunderball movie.

The *LCT* was used after WW II to carry freight to Exuma and back. One day, while running out of Nassau Harbor, she began to take on water. Her crew ran her aground on the north side of the island in an attempt to save the cargo.

Today, she sits in only four to 20 feet of water. Her hull is covered with fire coral, sponges, and sea fans. This is a nice dive, especially great for warming up on photography skills.

MAHONEY

The *Mahoney* was a 212 foot, steel hulled freighter that sank during a hurricane in 1929. This vessel was built in the 1880's and was renamed four times during her sailing days. None of these names were *Mahoney*, and it is still unknown how she became known as the *Mahoney* wreck. Originally named *Candance*, she sailed as a private yacht, as *Firequeen*, she served as a British admiralty flagship, as *Firebird*, she was used as a lighthouse tender and lastly as *Bahamian*, she was used as a freighter. The vessel was in tow to be scuttled and sold as scrap when she broke her tow line and sank off the western tip of Salt Key.

Today, known as the *Mahoney* wreck, she is scattered on a sandy bottom in 25 to 45 feet of water. She actually broke in two while sinking, so her bow and stern have been separated by about 100 yards. She was later blown up since it was decided she was a possible hazard to navigation. Water visibility here is usually a little cloudy, but on a clear day divers will have no problem finding her boilers which are located on the southwest side of her main wreckage. This wreck is covered with fire coral, so be sure to wear protective clothing. Her hull plates are also covered with gorgonians and corals and abound with a good assortment of marine life.

ROYAL JAMES

The *Royal James* wreck was an old Mississippi iron ferry, approximately 65 feet long. Her life as a ferry between Nassau and Paradise Island ended when the bridge was built. She was then used as a dive boat. In November of 1988, when old age would not permit anymore good use, local dive operators stripped and removed her engines, towed her out to sea and sunk her. She now sits in 45 feet of water close to the Golden Key drop off.

TEARS OF ALLAH

This 90 foot freighter is also known by the name of the *Never Say Never*

Bow of the *Tears of Allah* wreck also known as *Bond Wreck*. Photo courtesy A1 Forns.

Stern of the *Tears of Allah*. Photo courtesy Keith Ipson.

Again Wreck, or *Bond Wreck*. The *Tears of Allah* was a drug smuggler which was confiscated and later sold to movie producers. She was then sunk as a prop for a James Bond movie.

The wreck now sits in 45 feet of water, upright and intact, with a slight tilt to her port side. Al Forns, a skilled underwater photographer, says that the current at this site is almost non-existent, and visibility usually ranges from 80 to over 100 feet. This wreck is a great site for wide angle photography and can be especially exciting if you have an underwater video. *Tears of Allah* has also been used as a prop in a few TV commercials and in the movie Wet Gold.

VULCAN BOMBER

Only a few hundred yards from the *Tears of Allah* wreck lie the skeleton remains of a fighter jet prop used in the James Bond movie, Thunderball. The movie producers created the plane from steel pipe and a fiberglass coating. Today the fiberglass skin is gone, leaving what looks like a huge erector set sitting on the ocean bottom.

WILLAURIE

Ray Post says that this 130 foot mail boat that operated between Rum Cay,

The *WiLLaurie* washed hard onto the rocks, she was later refloated, towed to her present location and sunk. Photo courtesy Stephen Frink.

Stern of the *WiLLaurie*, notice her
original name *WiLMary* can still be
read. Photo courtesy Frazier Nivens.

Starboard side of the *WiLLaurie*. Photo courtesy Frazier Nivens.

San Sal and Cat Island originally sank in Potters Key, Nassau. The vessel which was initially a Danish Freighter, christened the *Will' Mary* was built back in 1907. She was raised from Potters Key and was in tow when a strong south wind picked up. While anchored, the winds became too strong for the mooring line which finally gave way. The *WiLLaurie* washed up hard onto the rocks. The ship was patched and re-floated once again, but this time the damage to her hull made the vessel unsalvageable. On December 26, 1988, Stuart Cove towed her to a spot just south of Goulding Key where she was sunk one final time.

The wreck is now lying in 50 feet of water. Her hull is upright, sitting on top of a reef. This recently sunk wreck has not had enough time to develop a full coat of marine growth, but it looks promising that one day she'll become an excellent dive site.

WRECK ON THE WALL

This confiscated drug runner was originally named the *Spiyva* but is now more commonly referred to as the *Wreck On The Wall* because of her resting location or *Cove's Rock Trawler*. She was a 41 foot wood trawler that was purchased from the government and sunk due south of the *Tears Of Allah* wreck.

Wreck of the Spiyva, better known as *Wreck on the Wall*. Photo courtesy Al Forns.

Wreck on the Wall.
Photo Keith Ipson.

The location and surroundings of the wreck make this site very unusual and interesting. As divers descend, they will find themselves on a coral wall that starts at 40 feet and plunges down to over 1,000 feet. The wreck's bow is actually hanging over the edge of this wall. Keith Ipson, an underwater photographer and N.Y. based dive shop owner, says that the combination of the wreck, the wall, and the abundance of fish and crustaceans makes this site very photogenic.

RUM CAY

Rum Cay is a small island, only four miles long by nine miles wide, with a population of less than a hundred. This island is not a busy, partying vacation spot. Instead, Rum Cay is a quiet, secluded, friendly island. In fact, there is only one paved road, 100 yards long on the island, and Rum Cay is rarely visited by more than 40 tourists at once. The name Rum Cay derived from a wrecked East Indian boat that lost its cargo of rum to the island's reefs.

Aside from the wreck we have listed, Rum Cay also offers divers many miles of shallow wall dives which are great for the novice as well as the more experienced diver.

H.M.S. CONQUEROR

The *H.M.S. Conqueror* was a 101 gun, screw line battleship. She was built in 1855 at the Davenport Dockyard, weighed 3,265 gross tons, was 240 feet long, and 55 feet wide. The *Conqueror* had 800 nhp steam engines that could push her at speeds of up to twelve knots. She was commissioned in 1856 for the Baltic Fleet and later the Mediterranean Fleet. She was armed with 36 eight inch shell guns, accurate to 1200 yards, 36 thirty two pound cannons, accurate to 2,000 yards, 28 thirty two pound upper deck guns which were less powerful than her other artillery but faster firing, and one 68 pound, ten foot long, eight inch bore pivot gun which was the most powerful gun of her day.

On December 12, 1861, while steaming from Port Royal, Jamaica to Bermuda, under the command of Captain E.S. Sotheby, she was carried 20 miles off course by a strong current. She ran aground and became stranded on Rum Cay. Fortunately, there was no loss of life. Her officers and crew made it safely ashore and constructed canvas shelters in which they lived until they were finally saved by a rescue ship. While the captain was acquitted of any blame, it was later attributed to the navigator.

101 Gun, screw line battleship *H.M.S. Conqueror.* Courtesy Steve Bielenda collection.

Painting of the *H.M.S. Conqueror* in a gale. Courtesy The Peabody Museum of Salem.

Diver explores the scattered remains of the warship *H.M.S. Conqueror*. Photo by Jozef Koppelman.

Wreckage of the *Conqueror*. Photo courtesy J.C. Laurier

Today, the wreck is located on the southeast side of Rum Cay, close to the entrance of Old Salt Lake, and lies in 15 to 25 feet of water. On this site, divers can find cannons, an anchor, a pile of lead bullets, and cannon balls. Artifacts cannot be taken from the wreck since she is protected by the Bahamian government.

According to Joe Koppelman, an instructor and experienced photographer, this wreck is surrounded by a forest of elkhorn coral, and is often visited by a nurse shark and a black tip reef shark (Carcharhings Limbatus).

SAN SALVADOR ISLAND

San Salvador is known as the island upon which Columbus made his first footstep in the new world. This island sits on top of the east edge of the Bahama bank and is located 175 miles east-southeast of Nassau.

This island has become quite attractive to divers. Especially nice for novice divers, there is no current with which to be concerned; the visibility is always excellent and the wall starts in only 35 feet of water and runs the whole 12 miles of the leeward side of the island.

SS FRASCATE

The *SS Frascate* was a 261 foot by 35 foot, English steel hulled freighter. The *Frascate* was built in 1886 in Germany and originally named *Daszig*. On January 1, 1902, while en route from New York to Jamaica, she ran aground and sunk.

Today, the *Frascate* lies scattered on a sandy bottom in 15 to 20 feet of water off Riding Rock Point. She was blown apart by the Army Corp of Engineers as she was believed to be a hazard to navigation, and has since then been spread over a very large area.

Her two large steam boilers remain intact and are the highest points on the wreck. Other recognizable items include deck plating, a pile of anchor chain and ballast stones. Her wreckage has become home to many small crabs, sergeant majors, and a green moray eel that lives in the boiler. Divers can actually swim through a 20 foot tunnel formation that runs the entire length of her massive boiler. The *Frascate's* stern section is excellent for photography. Her bow still holds some of the ship's cargo of flour which remain neatly stacked in sacks that have over time become a concrete like substance.

Frascate wreck. Photo
by Stephen Frink.

PORT KEMBELA

The *Port Kembela*, also known as the *Port Campbell*, was a 474 foot freighter. She ran aground in 1924 and remained intact until a hurricane broke her up in 1926.

She is now resting outside of a reef in 25 feet of water on a hard rock bottom. The *Port Kembela* is only accessible on very calm days due to the swells and a strong surge that is common in the area.

CARIBBEAN

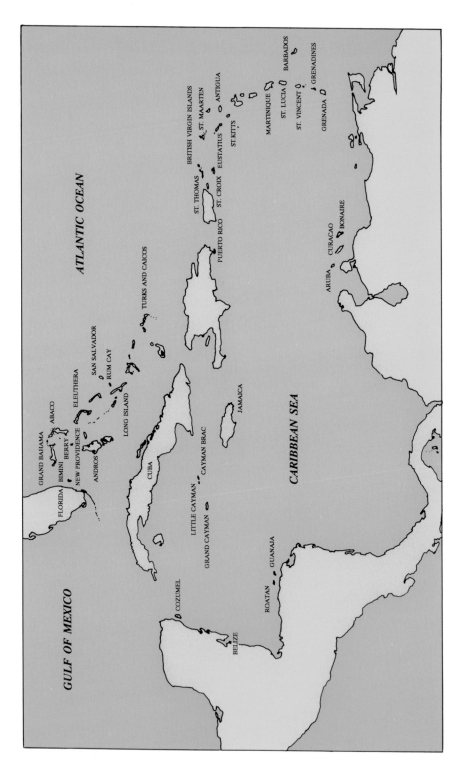

GULF OF MEXICO

ATLANTIC OCEAN

CARIBBEAN SEA

FLORIDA
GRAND BAHAMA
BIMINI
BERRY
NEW PROVIDENCE
ANDROS
ABACO
ELEUTHERA
SAN SALVADOR
RUM CAY
LONG ISLAND
TURKS AND CAICOS
CUBA
LITTLE CAYMAN
GRAND CAYMAN
CAYMAN BRAC
JAMAICA
COZUMEL
BELIZE
ROATAN
GUANAJA
PUERTO RICO
ST. THOMAS
ST. CROIX
BRITISH VIRGIN ISLANDS
EUSTATIUS
ST. MAARTEN
ST. KITTS
ANTIGUA
MARTINIQUE
ST. LUCIA
BARBADOS
ST. VINCENT
GRENADINES
GRENADA
ARUBA
CURACAO
BONAIRE

40

ANTIGUA **British Leeward Islands**

Antigua was originally settled by the British in 1632. In 1981 the island gained independence, and now its economy is supported by a growing tourist trade. Antigua offers not only great diving with an abundance of reefs and fish, but nightlife, casinos, dancing and duty free shopping. Antigua also has hundreds of shipwrecks, most of which are still waiting to be discovered.

ANDES

The *Andes* was a British Bark under the command of Captain Griffith. She sank in deep bay on June 5, 1905. Apparently, the vessel caught fire and blew up while en route from Trinidad to Valparaiso. At the time of her demise, she was carrying a full cargo of asphalt in barrels. The vessel and cargo were a total loss, but her crew was saved.

The wreck remains upright in 30 feet of water. Divers can descend through her open decks or swim around her exterior. Snorkelers as well as divers often visit the *Andes*. Some marine life is present here but is not as abundant as it is at some of the other off shore sites.

ST. JOHN WRECK

The *St. John Wreck* is also referred to as *Shipstern*. She was a 90 foot long tug boat that sank in St. James harbor in the 1960's. The wreck is now resting in about 35 feet of water. The *St. John Wreck* is great for wide angle photography. Due to the amount of small crustaceans and colorful coral polyps, this site is also an impressive night dive.

About sixty feet behind the *St. John Wreck* is a barge wreck. It is not known if both vessels were sunk together or if they each went down during unconnected incidences.

ARUBA **Netherland Antilles**

Aruba is the most westerly of the ABC islands of the Netherlands Antilles, lying 15 miles north of Venezuela. The island is well known for its white sand beaches, casinos and resorts.

Most diving is done off the island's west coast, and there are a number of interesting and historic shipwrecks to be explored.

Aruba

Stern of the *Antilla*, sunk in May of 1940. This wreck is also known as the *Ghost Ship*. Photo courtesy Aruba Tourism Board.

Antilla wreck. Photo courtesy Aruba Tourism Board.

ANTILLA

The *Antilla*, also known as the *German Freighter Wreck*, or *Ghost Ship*, was 397 feet long, had a 55.4 foot beam, weighed 2,164 net tons, and 4,400 gross tons. She was built in 1939 by Finkenwarder at Hamburg and was powered by two steam turbines. Although she was a brand new German vessel, the *Antilla* was sunk intentionally but not to make a dive site or fish haven. She was an unarmed ship used by the Germans to supply their submarines during WW II and was nick-named *Ghost Ship* by the allies who were never able to locate and attack the ship outside of neutral waters. When Germany invaded Holland in May of 1940, the *Antilla* was moored just off the shore of Aruba which is a Dutch territory. The local law enforcement immediately asked for her surrender but gave her captain a day to think about it. That night the *Antilla* was scuttled in order to prevent the ship's capture. Her captain and crew were detained for the rest of the war in a prisoner of war camp on the island of Bonaire.

The *Antilla* now rests in 50 to 60 feet of water off the south side of Aruba. She is one of the largest wrecks in the Caribbean and rests intact on a sand bottom. This dive is very interesting for beginner and experienced divers alike. Due to the large compartments of this vessel, this is a great wreck for penetration. Many of these compartments are unopened, and, therefore, remain unexplored. Visibility is good but not great, averaging 30 to 60 feet. Marine life is abundant on the wreck, and she is covered with giant tube sponges and coral formations. The *Antilla* is also surrounded by rock lobsters and all other types of tropical fish. Night dives at this site are great for macro photography. Many little critters can be found to photograph, including banded coral shrimp, arrow crabs, and hermit crabs.

SS CALIFORNIA

This wreck is known as the *SS California*. Many magazine articles and reference sources have listed this wreck as being the remains of the ship that received but did not respond to the *Titanic's* S.O.S. signal. In fact, the vessel involved with the *Titanic* disaster was a 447 foot long, steel hulled Leyland Liner that was torpedoed off Cape Matapan on November 9th, 1915. The ship involved with the *Titanic* was named *Californian* not *California*, and is definitely not this wood hulled wreckage lying off Aruba.

However, this unidentified shipwreck is fascinating to explore and is located at a depth that makes it very convenient for underwater photography, only 15 to 30 feet. The wreck is located on the northwest tip of Aruba where at times a strong current is present. If divers swim out past the wreck into deeper water, there's a good chance of seeing bull or hammerhead sharks.

JANE SEA

The *Jane Sea* is the latest underwater attraction in Aruba. She is a 170 foot long, English freighter which was scuttled in September of 1988 in order to form a fish haven. The *Jane Sea* is the most intact wreck off the island, and lies in 60 to 100 feet of water near Barcadera Reef. She is engulfed by a sandy bottom with brain coral formations and an abundance of huge sea fans of different species everywhere. Plenty of incredible encounters with marine life await you at this breathtaking dive site.

PEDERNALES

Just a little south from the *Antilla* wreck lies another casualty of war. The *Pedernales* wreck is the remains of a torpedoed oil tanker. As the story goes, the bow and stern sections of the ship were sealed, cut off, salvaged and fitted onto another vessel which was later employed in the Normandy invasion of WW II.

Today, this wreck, which is just the center section of a once proud vessel, lies in 25 to 40 feet of water in front of the Holiday Inn Hotel. It is a beginner diver's paradise offering a combination of large pieces of wreckage spread out between coral formations as well as completely intact wreck cabins. Divers will see everything from wash basins, lavatories, and toilets to two torpedoes. Due to the shallow depth and clear water of this wreck, she can be enjoyed by snorkelers as well as divers.

The colorful coral encrusted bow of the *Tugboat* wreck. Photo courtesy Aruba Tourism Board.

TUGBOAT WRECK

This is a super dive site. As divers descend to the wreck, they will start to see magnificent formations of brain coral, star coral and sheet coral. Gradually, the remains of this old tug boat will emerge from the distance. Usually a pair of green morays will await your arrival. I've been told that it is not uncommon to see spotted eagle rays and sting rays in the same vicinity. This site is a favorite of many photographers.

BARBADOS   Southern Caribbean

Although comparatively small, this island is one of the most populated and developed in the Caribbean.

Barbados diving is known for its wreck sites and reef formations. However, due to the enormous amount of fishing done off the island, large fish are seldom seen by divers.

BERWYN

This 60 foot French tug boat sank in 1919 off the south coast of Barbados. Today, she sits upright and intact in 20 to 25 feet of water, only 100 yards from shore. This site is often used as a training dive for scuba or resort courses. The intact iron structure is heavily encrusted with coral, allows for easy penetration, and portrays a classic shipwreck background for wide angle photography. A local dive operator has set up a fish feeding station on the site, so be sure to bring some food for the local inhabitants.

FRIAR'S CRAIG

This vessel, according to Willie Hassell, owner of Willie's Watersports, is a 160 foot long steamer that was scuttled intentionally in 1985 to form a fish haven. She sits in 50 feet of water and has already attracted a nice assortment of fish.

PAMIR

The *Pamir* wreck is a 155 foot freighter that was also intentionally scuttled in 1985 to attract fish. She lies completely intact in 50 feet of water about 100 yards offshore. Located on the northwest side of the island, this wreck can be visited by boat, or divers can reach her by swimming from the beach.

STAVRONIKITA

The *Stavronikita* is probably the most popular wreck on Barbados. She was a 365 foot Greek freighter built in Denmark in 1956 and originally christened the *Ohio*. On August 26, 1976, while en route from Ireland to the Caribbean and carrying a cargo of 101,000 bags of cement, the vessel caught fire, killing six crew members and injuring three others. An explosion that folowed the fire destroyed all of the ship's radio equipment, making it impossible for the stranded crew to call for help. Twenty four crewmen drifted in the open sea for four days before being rescued. The *Stavronikita* was then towed to Barbados.

A year went by, and the vessel was still anchored off Carlisle Bay, Barbados. On October 24, 1977, she was purchased at an auction for the sum of $30,000 by the Parks and Beach Commission. The ship was then stripped of all the machinery and brass that could be salvaged. She was cleaned of pollutants, namely the 70,000 gallons of oil being carried in her fuel tanks and towed to a spot just 400 yards offshore on the west coast of the island. On November 21, 1978, the U.S. Navy demolition crew set seven charges totalling 200 pounds and blew holes in the ship's hull, causing her to sink.

Stavronikita after the fire. Note the SOS painted on her hull in an attempt to summon help to the stranded crew. Photo courtesy W.M. Schell, negative by Charles F. Schell.

Today, the huge wreck *Stavronikita* rests in 20 to 130 feet of water. Exploration around and inside her pilot house, down passageways, or up by her bow where the vessel's name can still be read is something that divers should not miss.

BELIZE   **Western Caribbean**

Belize is located along the eastern shore of Central America and borders the Caribbean sea. Belize is a melting pot comprised of immigrants from South and Central America, Africa, India, the Mideast, Asia, West Indies, and lastly Americans. The Mayan indians have left behind many archeological sites that mark their existence between 1500 B.C. and 1000 A.D. when they mysteriously disappeard. The coast is a lowland with marshes, swamps, and lagoons.

Ranging from ten to 30 miles off shore lies the barrier reef. Due to the crystal clear waters, coral gardens, sand and sea grass bottom, some of the largest reef fish and shellfish in the Caribbean can be found here. Divers should also visit the coral atolls surrounding Belize such as Turneffe Reef, and Glover's Reef.

Bow of the *Sayonara,* a wood hulled transport sunk in 1983. Photo courtesy Stephen Frink.

The name *Sayonara* is still visible on her stern. Photo courtesy Stephen Frink.

47

CHANGA'S WRECK

Changa's Wreck is the busted up remains of an old wooden barge. She sits in 10 feet of water and is home to a nice variety of fish, including an occasional stingray.

SAYONARA

The 50 foot long wreck of the *Sayonara* was a wood hulled transport vessel sunk in 1983. She is now sitting in 45 to 50 feet of water very close to a wall. The name *Sayonara* is still visible on her stern section.

The wreck does not seem to attract too much in the way of marine life but is, however, a pretty wreck to take pictures of. Wide angle 15 or 20mm bow photos are nice. Getting your buddy to enter her wheel house while taking photographs through her window openings can result in some great shots.

BONAIRE   Netherland Antilles

Bonaire is the most arid of the Caribbean islands and lies 50 miles north of Venezuela. Within the island's crystal blue waters are a protected Marine Park that will ensure that the underwater environment remains unspoiled for generations to come.

This 100 foot long barge was sunk in 1972. Photo by Chip Cooper.

Due to the easy access and abundance of dive sites, excellent visibility, sloping coral reefs and large assortment of marine life, Bonaire is considered by many to contain the best diving in the world. As we found on our trip, every shipwreck and every reef abounds with colorful and friendly marine life which include angelfish, sea horses, large groupers, jacks, and lobsters.

COOPERS BARGE

This barge wreck, nicknamed *Coopers Barge*, was sunk in 1972. Although an attempt was made to salvage this completely intact sunken barge, the operation resulted only in accidentally relocating the barge to deeper water. The *Barge* can be found directly in front of the desalinization plant on Bonaire, and this dive can only be done when a tanker is not off loading fuel. To find the 100 foot long wreck, you have to tie up to the southern most mooring and then swim about 100 yards north. She is sitting in deep water, 130 to 140 feet.

HESPER

The *Hesper* was a 40 foot long, wood sailboat that had been purchased by Captain Don of Captain Don's Habitat for 300 gilders, or about 150 American dollars. She was moored in front of the Habitat, undergoing a complete overhaul that included a new mast when Hurricane Gilbert ripped past the area. After the storm, the *Hesper* was gone. She is now lying in 130 feet of water on a sandy bottom.

HILMA HOOKER

The *Hilma Hooker* was a 236 foot long cargo vessel weighing 1,027 gross tons registered in San Andres, Columbia. She was originally named the *Midsland* when she was built in Holland in 1951. The vessel was later renamed *Mistral, William Express, Anna, Doric Express* and finally *Hilma Hooker*.

The *Hilma Hooker* ran into some mechanical rudder difficulties while passing the island of Bonaire. She was taken in tow and brought to the town pier, where customs immigration officials decided to search her after discovering that she carried no papers. It was soon learned that the FBI had been tracking the vessel by satellite on the suspicion that she was transporting illegal drugs. What they found on the *Hilma Hooker* was over 25,000 pounds of marijuana hidden behind a false bulkhead. The marijuana was confiscated, taken out of town and burned.

The *Hooker* remained tied up to the town pier for months while officials

Rare photograph of the *Hilma Hooker* sinking. Courtesy Andre Nahr.

tried to locate the vessel's owner. After a while she was moved and moored just offshore. Her hull, which was not in the best condition, began to take on water, and her pumps eventually gave out. On the morning of September 12, 1984, at approximately 9:00 AM, the vessel rolled over and sank.

Not too long after her sinking, local dive operators got together and took actions that made the *Hilma Hooker* a safe wreck for sport divers. They opened doors, cut cables, and drilled holes into the wreck's port side. The holes provided a way for air, generated from divers breathing on scuba to escape. This was done so no one would be tempted to remove their regulator while in a trapped air pocket, since air in these pockets is usually oxygen depleted from the rusting steel. Al Catalfumo, owner of a local dive operation, says that he and his partner cut a cable that was holding the vessel's cargo door open; if left alone it would have deteriorated and snapped, possibly when divers were under these huge doors. Al went on to say that the door fell with such force that visibility was instantly reduced to zero as the wreck was enveloped in a cloud of sand.

The *Hilma Hooker* now sits on her starboard side in 90 feet of water. She is completely intact and absolutely beautiful to dive as well as to photograph. Her large bronze propeller sits in 65 feet of water. She has a stern helm which is excellent for photos and, due to the usual amount of good ambient light, wide angle photographs result in nice bow and stern shots. The *Hooker* has also turned into a good fish haven. Her rusting structure is refuge to

The *Hooker's* bow is ideal for wide angle photography. Photo by Daniel Berg.

The *Hilma Hooker* sits on her starboard side in 90 feet of water. She is completely intact and absolutely beautiful to dive on as well as photograph. Photo courtesy Jozef Koppelman.

The *Hooker's* engine room. Penetration of any wreck should only be done by divers with proper training. Photo by Chip Cooper.

all types of sea creatures, large and small alike.

As a side note, the *Hilma Hooker* wreck is lying just next to a coral reef. This is an ideal location because divers can spend a good amount of time on the wreck, and then slowly ascend while exploring the reef. This extends bottom time exploration, while divers are still out gassing.

LA MACHACA

This small fishing boat was originally sunk in 120 feet of water and then

The upside down remains of the *La Machaca*. Photo by Chip Cooper.

relocated as a dive site and fish haven. She is now lying upside down in 33 feet of water in front of Captain Don's Habitat. The wreck is home to a large tiger grouper and a pair of black margates.

MARI BAHN

The *Mari Bahn*, which is Gaelic for *Bonny Mary*, was known for years as the *Deep Schooner*, or the *Wind Jammer* wreck. This three masted iron bark, owned by Fratelli Denegri and G.B. Mortola, was built in 1874 by Barclay, Curle and Company, Glasgow, Scotland. She was schooner rigged on the mizzen mast, fore and aft, and square rigged on the others. She was 239 feet long, had a 37 foot beam, and weighed 1,378 gross tons. At the time of her demise, she was sailing under the command of Captain L. Razeto from Trinidad to Marseille with a cargo of asphalt. The date of her sinking was December 7, 1912.

According to photo journalist Cathy Cush, she is sunk in 200 feet of water off the northwest coast of the island, just off the old oil terminal. The wreck is too deep for sport divers to explore but is visited on occasion by experienced professional divers. Photographer Chip Cooper says that her foremast rests in 35 feet of water and points the way towards her deeper hull. She lies on her starboard side with the top of her port side in 160 feet. Her main mast and crows nest extend down to 220 feet.

This rare historical photograph is one of the only topside photos in existence of the *Mari Bahn*. Courtesy Chip Cooper collection.

Bonaire

Frank Valenti explores and photographs the Mari Bahn wreck, better known as the *Wind Jammer* or *Deep Schooner*. Photo courtesy Jozef Koppelman.

Charlie Guttilla and partners near the *Wind Jammer's* bowsprit. Photo courtesy Jozef Koppelman

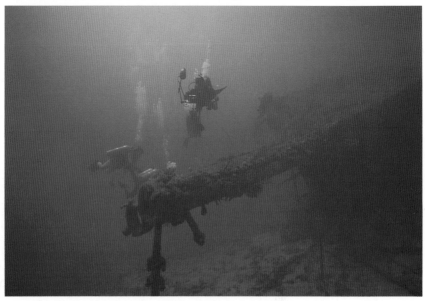

This picture perfect little tug is resting on her port side in 70 feet of water. Photo courtesy Herb Segars.

TUG

This picture perfect little wreck is located directly in front of the Bonaire Scuba Center. She was originally named the *Cavalier State* but is more commonly referred to as the *Tug*. She is resting on her port side in 60 to 70 feet of water and is home to an exceptionally large moray eel. She is an excellent beach dive, and is visited by thousands of divers each year. Photographer, Herb Segars, says the *Tug* is resting on a sand bottom and is excellent for macro as well as wide angle shots.

BRITISH VIRGIN ISLANDS   B.V.I.

Comprised of over 40 islands and located just east of the U.S. Virgin Islands, the British Virgin Islands are a wreck diver's dream location. One of the most famous shipwrecks in the Caribbean, the *Rhone* is just one example of the incredible number of wrecks located in this area. Anegada alone, a submerged reef system, has claimed hundreds of ships over the past century. Many of these wrecks, especially the ones located on Anegada, are hard for sport divers to reach because the treacherous shallow reefs, which caused the demise of so many fine vessels, could just as easily claim a dive boat. For that reason, many potential dive sites have remained unexplored.

Two pork fish amid masts and rigging of the *Chikuzen*. Photo by James B. Scheiner.

Stern of the Korean refrigerator ship
Chikuzen which sank on August 12,
1981. Photo courtesy James B. Scheiner,
Rainbow Visions Photography.

Two cobia swim through the *Chikuzen's* rigging. Photo courtesy James B. Scheiner, Rainbow Visions
Photography.

CHIKUZEN

This, 223 foot long, Korean refrigerator ship was one of a fishing fleet operating in the area at the time of her sinking. She was built in 1960 in Japan and originally named *Seiju Mau #1*. According to Jim Scheiner, underwater photographer and owner of Rainbow Visions Photography, the vessel's engines stopped working, but the Korean fishing fleet was still able to make good use of her refrigeration. On August 11, 1981, the fleet received word that a storm was coming. The vessel had to be moved from its dock, so the owners towed it out and tried to scuttle her. They set the ship on fire, but she didn't sink. The *Chikuzen* drifted overnight and caused some locals to worry since they thought she was going to end up on the beach. A tug boat towed the ship to her present location about seven miles north of Tortola before the 240 foot vessel finally sank.

The *Chikuzen* is now resting on her port side in 75 feet of water and has become a popular site for traveling divers. Her intact structure is not yet heavily developed with marine growth, but huge schools of snappers, jacks, barracuda, parrot fish, grunts, spade fish and groupers are some of the local inhabitants. Lots of big fish can also be seen in the area such as amberjack, eagle rays, and an occasional black tip reef shark.

FEARLESS

The wreck of the *Fearless*, a 70 foot long fishing trawler, lies intact in

Cabin of the *Fearless*. Photo courtesy Chip Cooper.

about 80 feet of water just off Peter Island. She sank in 1986 due to old age and poor upkeep. According to diver Chip Cooper, a large section of her starboard aft hull loosened and down she went.

HAULOVER BAY

This unidentified fishing trawler burned and sank off of Cooper's Island around 1985. She is about 60 feet long and rests on a sand bottom in 60 feet of water.

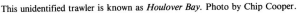

This unidentified trawler is known as *Houlover Bay*. Photo by Chip Cooper.

R.M.S. RHONE

The *Rhone* was built by the Millwall Iron Works of England. She was 310 feet long, had a 40 foot beam, and weighed 2,738 gross tons. This Royal Mail Steamer had 253 first class, 30 second class and 30 third class cabins. Powered by both sail and steam, she was fitted with a 500 hp compound steam engine that could push the vessel at a top speed of 14 knots.

During her two years of service for the Royal Mail Steam Packet Company, the *Rhone* carried mail, passengers, and general cargo. It was on her tenth voyage that this sleek ship met her doom. At 11:00 AM October 29, 1867, the *Rhone* was lying at anchor off Peter Island when the ship's barometer began to fall fast and the sky turned black. As the wind and sea got wilder,

Divers explore the *R.M.S. Rhone's* boiler. Photo by Chip Cooper.

Bob Doheny points to a cannon pinned under the *Rhone's* bow section. Photo courtesy Chip Cooper.

Captain Wooley put her engines at full speed ahead in an effort to steam to her anchor and ride out the storm. During this hour, a spar fell from her rigging, killing first officer, Mr. Topper. During a lull in the storm, Captain Wooley decided to weigh anchor to gain open sea, but while trying to hoist the vessels 3,000 pound anchor, a shackle got caught in the hawser pipe and broke. Her anchor plus about 300 feet of chain were lost. Finally, the *Rhone* steamed out towards sea at full power, but before she could make a clean getaway, the hurricane swept back and down hard, forcing her stern first onto the rocks of Tortola. The ship soon broke in two taking with her 123 out of 145 passengers and crew to their watery grave.

Besides losing the *Rhone* and most of her crew, the Royal Mail Steam Packet Company also lost the vessels, *Derwent* and *Wye*. Two other ships, the *Solent* and *Tyne*, were heavily damaged. No other shipping company to date has ever sustained such a loss of ships in the course of a single day. Of the 60 vessels at anchor around St. Thomas and the neighboring islands, only two survived the severity of this storm.

Today, the *Rhone* is a Marine Park designated "*R.M.S. Rhone* National Park". Taking of artifacts, coral or shells is prohibited. Her bow rests in 90 feet of water and points north. The bow section is mostly intact, lying on its starboard side. Her foremast and crows' nest are intact, and one of her cannons lies under some wreckage in 70 feet. The wrecks stern lies perpendicular to her bow and slopes up to shallower water, while the depth of the aft section ranges from 20 to 80 feet. Any diver who has ever visited this wreck will surely rave about this experience. Divers can still see portholes, winches, her boilers, a large set of open end wrenches, her propeller and bow sprit.

ROCUS

The *Rocus* was a Greek cargo vessel that ran aground and sank near Anegada. At the time of her sinking, the *Rocus* was transporting a very

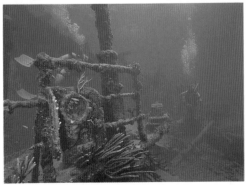

The Greek cargo vessel *Rocus,* better known as the *Bone Wreck.* Photo courtesy Nancy Sefton.

interesting cargo of cow bones. The *Rocus* was en route to deliver these bones to a fertilizer factory when she met her demise.

Today the wreck is very broken up in 15 to 35 feet of water. Her rubble and thousands of bones are scattered over a large area. Some divers refer to this site as the *Graveyard Wreck* or *Bone Wreck* and have reported an eerie feeling while exploring the wreckage on night dives.

CAYMAN BRAC   Cayman Islands

Cayman Brac is considered by many seasoned travelers to be the most beautiful island in the Caymans. Cayman Brac's most outstanding geographical feature is its 130 foot high limestone bluff, which runs from its west end to its east end. Brac diving is usually done on the north side due to a more rugged and rough south side.

CAYMAN MARINER

This is the newest wreck to sink in the waters off of Cayman Brac. The *Cayman Mariner* was a 65 foot long vessel operated by Cayman Energy Limited. Originally used as a tender to transport crews to and from oil tankers, the *Mariner* was intentionally sunk as a dive site in September of 1986.

The *Cayman Mariner* is now resting in 50 to 60 feet of water. According to veteran diver, Craig Burns, this wreck is an excellent photo prop for divers, and visibility is usually excellent, ranging from 100 to over 200 feet.

KISSIME

The *Kissime* is a great little wreck of a 60 foot tug boat. She was sunk back in 1982 and lies intact on a sand bottom in 35 to 40 feet of water. The wreck is leaning on her port side and is surrounded by a beautiful reef. The average visibility here ranges from 80 to 120 feet. The *Kissime* is a favorite spot for wide angle photography as well as video.

PRINCE FREDERICK

The *Prince Frederick* was a 110 foot, wood hulled, twin masted vessel. She was powered by both steam and sail and is said to have sunk in the late 1800's. Her remains lie on the south side of Cayman Brac in 20 to 40 feet of water.

The silhouetted bow of the *Cayman Mariner* sunk in 1986. Photo courtesy Keith Ipson.

The *Kissime* is a favorite spot for wide angle photography as well as video. Photo courtesy Jozef Koppelman.

Although most of her wood hull has been destroyed by teredos (wood eating worms), parts of her machinery and masts can still be seen. Divers who visit the site will find piles of anchor chain, four anchors, the wrecks boilers, and some remaining wood beams.

COZUMEL MEXICO

Of Mexico's Caribbean islands, Cozumel is the largest, extending 28 miles long by 11 miles wide. This Mexican island lies 12 miles off the coast of the Yucatan Peninsula.

Most Cozumel diving is drift diving done along the reef wall off the island's west coast. The reef is inhabited by sharks, eels, scorpionfish and barracudas. Inside the reef are many caves and tunnels to be explored.

AIRPLANE WRECK

The *Airplane Wreck* was a 40 passenger, twin engine, short-range *Convair* airliner. The craft, which was built by the Convair Division of the General Dynamics Corporation, was deliberately sunk in June of 1977 as a movie prop for the Mexican movie "Survive II".

The *Plane* wreck is now a tourist attraction, that is if the tourists are

This upside down Convair airliner was sunk deliberately in June, 1977. Photo by Daniel Berg.

Denise Berg peers into the planes engine cavity, notice the landing gear. Photo by Daniel Berg.

divers. She is lying upside down in 40 feet of water, only 100 yards out from the La Ceiba Hotel. This wreck is an easy beach dive and has remained remarkably intact. Divers can enter a small area through an open door just aft of her cockpit or swim under either of her wings where small schools of tropical fish can usually be found. Her hull is cleaned daily by parrot fish who leave deep teeth marks in her fuselage. Wide angle photography is best here, and you can easily capture the entire wreck on one photo.

DEL MAR WRECK

The *Del Mar Wreck* is the remains of a small, wood hulled fishing boat approximately 30 feet long. The wreck is located directly in front of Del Mar Aquatics and rests in 30 to 40 feet of water on a sand bottom.

CURACAO   Netherland Antilles

Curacao is the middle ABC island and lies 35 miles north of Venezuela. The port of Williamstad lures more than a quarter of a million cruise ship tourists a year, and this doesn't include the large amount of other tourists. Curacao is the center of the ABC island's government and is more heavily populated and industrious than its sister islands.

Since the diving in Curacao has only recently become popular, divers will find the coral formations are in excellent condition. Aside from the untouched marine life, Curacao offers colorful wall dives and steep, sloping drop offs.

SUPERIOR PRODUCER

The *Superior Producer* was a 200 foot, steel hulled freighter. In October of 1977, she was about to begin her voyage from St. Anna bay, Curacao to Venezuela. Immediately after leaving the harbor, she began to take on water, listed and sank. At the time of her demise, the *Producer* was carrying a mixed cargo that consisted of liquor, clothing, perfume, luggage and wallets.

Within hours, local divers were in the water diving as many as six times in one day to salvage all they could from the *Producer's* cargo. Unfortunately, many of these divers lacked deep diving experience and many ended up with the bends as safe diving rules were ignored. As the story goes, it was the liquor that was harvested first, and there turned out to be some party that night.

The freighter now rests on a sand bottom in 110 feet of water where the current is sometimes strong. Sitting upright and intact, the top of her wheel house is in 80 feet, and her bridge is in 90 feet of water. A toilet can be found in the room next to the bridge; this spot makes an interesting photo opportunity. Just be careful of the fire coral on the rim of the seat. Visibility ranges from 100 to 150 feet.

A large green moray eel has made the deck winch of the *Superior Producer* his home. Also seen in the area of the wreck have been large manta rays and schools of barracuda consisting of twenty to thiry fish.

TOWBOAT

This tiny wreck, which is also known as the *Tug Boat* wreck is only about a mile away from the wreck of the *Superior Producer*. The *Towboat* is a 25 foot tug boat that looks exactly like any larger tug, only miniaturized. The wreck is in the Curacao Underwater Park and is sitting upright on a white sandy bottom in only 17 feet of water. The *Towboat* is a very popular dive for beginners as well as snorkelers. Experienced underwater photographers also visit this site to shoot both wide angle and macro shots. Some of the nicer macro photos are of black sea horses that are sometimes found on the wreck. Divers will find her wheel house an ideal location for pictures.

This tiny tugboat rests in only 17 feet of water in the Curacao Underwater Park. Photo courtesy Curacao Department of Tourism.

The *Anna Marie*. Photo
by Courtney Platt ©.

GRAND CAYMAN
Cayman Islands

Grand Cayman is the largest and principal island of the Caymans. The island is known for its beautiful beaches, especially "Seven Mile Beach". Watersports to be found here include scuba diving, snorkeling, jet skiing, sailing, water skiing, submarine rides, and para sailing, to mention a few. Grand Cayman is one of the best known dive locations in the Caribbean, and each time we visit this paradise in the sun, we gain more respect for the beauty hidden beneath the blue Cayman waters.

ANNA MARIE

The *Anna Marie* is also referred to as the *Tug Wreck*. She was a 25 foot long, wood hulled tugboat that was used as a support vessel for the Atlantis submarine. The little tug was sunk by a storm in 1987 and now rests upright in 50 feet of water on a sand flat just outside of Devil's Grotto in the southwest corner of Georgetown Harbor. This miniature tug has now been transformed into a wonderful little fish haven and makes a great background for wide angle photographs.

BALBOA

The *Balboa* was a 375 foot freighter sunk, on November 10th, 1932, during a hurricane. After sailing from Cuba into Georgetown, the ship began to experience engine trouble. She was then caught in shallow water while enduring a hurricane in full force. Mother nature played a cruel trick on the *Balboa* by inflicting waves so high that the ship was bounced up and down off the ocean floor. Eventually, the vessel could take no more, and her hull gave way.

The *Balboa* was carrying a cargo of wood and oil when she went down. The Caymanians claim that after the ship sunk you could have walked from the wreck to shore on her cargo of wood without even getting your feet wet. It is also said that the wood that washed onto shore was used to build a church steeple. The story of this wreck is told by dive masters as being a gift from God.

In 1957, the Army Corp. of Engineers decided that this wreck was a hazard to navigation, and had to be blown up.

Today, the *Balboa* rests on a sandy bottom in 30 to 35 feet of water. Divers can explore her stern section which remains partially intact, or they can swim over a large three bladed steel propeller. Divers can also swim

Divers on the stern section of the *Balboa*. Photo courtesy Courtney Platt © 1989

Balboa's three bladed steel propeller. Photo by Courtney Platt © 1989.

through a tent like shape that was formed by her steel hull plates.

Fish feeding and photography are ideal activities for this wreck. The *Balboa* seems to attract a large array of aquatic life. We were lucky enough to find and photograph a large green moray eel in the *Balboa's* boiler room, located just off the wreck's starboard side. Also happy to have their picture taken were some tiger groupers. This site has become a quite popular night dive too. According to noted photographer Joe Koppleman, the *Balboa* is one of the best places in the world to find and photograph the Orange Ball

Anonyme (Pseudocorynactis Caribbeorun). Also called Sunburst Anonyme, this rare species is seldom seen by divers.

CALLIE

Built in 1900, the *Callie* wreck was a 220 foot, four masted steel schooner, or barkentine that had been refitted with an engine. The *Callie* was said to have been carrying a cargo of grain when she ran aground in 1944. As the grain absorbed sea water that was leaking in, it quickly expanded and caused the doom of the ship. Since the *Callie* had become a serious hazard to navigation in the area, it was decided in 1957, as it was with the *Balboa*, that the British Army Corp of Engineers would blow her up. The *Callie* now lies scattered over a very large area just inshore from the *Balboa* and about 100 feet from shore in 20 feet of water.

Since the wreckage is so close to shore, access is very easy for anyone interested. She is located directly in front of "Surfside Watersports" where divers may conveniently rent gear and tanks. You can then swim to the *Callie* from the beach by following a 300 degree compass course. The shop owners have placed steps in the water which make for an easy entry from their deck. There are also various boat trips that can be taken to the *Callie*. Boat loads of snorkelers can explore not only the wreck but the surrounding reef as well. If you're diving on the wreck when one of these boats arrive as we were, this area will suddenly look like the sea of legs.

Daniel Berg exploring the bow of the *Callie*. Photo by Denise Berg.

While a diver is approaching the *Callie* which is marked with a large steel mooring buoy, the first piece to be seen is a large triangular shaped portion of her bow. This introduction to the wreck only makes you more enthusiastic about ending this rather long swim and finally reaching the main wreckage area. Slightly north of this piece is the main area. Once you get there, you'll see pieces of the broken ship everywhere you look. In fact, it's hard to decide which way to go first. Although less obvious than the rest of the wreck, divers can easily locate a huge pile of anchor chain. Next you will come across her large deck winch, then swimming along the keel to her massive engine and partially intact stern section. Observant divers should be able to locate an intact porthole that is lying face down still firmly attached to a steel plate.

The marine life at this wreck was not as impressive as the other wrecks on the island, but we did see some large barracuda, tiger groupers, two large puffer fish, trumpet fish, a small spotted moray eel, and , of course, the always present and ready for a handout, yellow tailed snappers. Don't forget about the reef surrounding the wreck. As we found out, it is definitely worth exploring, and since you're diving in such shallow water a full tank of air allows plenty of time to explore both the wreck and the reef.

CARRIE LEE

The *Carrie Lee* was a freighter approximately 100 feet in length that originally sank on the far side of Grand Cayman. While en route, the ship capsized, turtled, and floated upside down for a few days. In an attempt to save her, she was towed into Georgetown, but this attempt was in vain. The *Carrie Lee* sunk, flipped over again, and landed on the bottom upright and intact.

Unfortunately for the local dive operations, the *Carrie Lee* didn't stay in water shallow enough for sport divers. Instead, she slid down a sandy slope to her present location which puts her stern in 130 feet of water and her bow in approximately 200 feet of water.

We were lucky enough to be able to charter two dive trips to the *Carrie Lee*. On our first trip, we scouted the wall for about 20 minutes in search of the wreck and finally found her. Unfortunately our bottom time was used up, and we had no choice but to settle for a distant photo. Exploration was left for another day.

On our second trip, Captain Butch brought us right to the wreck. We found her to be perfectly intact, and it looked as though she was waiting

The *Carrie Lee* capsized and floated upside down before sinking during an attempt to right her, Photo by Courtney Platt © 1989.

The bow of the *Carrie Lee* is now resting on a sand and coral sloping seabed in 200 feet of water. Photo courtesy Courtney Platt © 1989.

"Carrie Lee, Grand Turk" can still be read on the stern of this wreck. Photo by Courtney Platt © 1989.

for us to explore her rusted remains. Her pilot house is accessible through a door on her port side. A big spotlight and brass horns are still mounted atop the pilot house. If we swam any further ahead of the pilot house, we would have ended up in water considered too deep for sport divers. However, we were totally in our glory just to be able to explore the stern section since there was such a large assortment of interesting items. Among these items was an intact porthole and, after wiping off some light marine growth, we were able to read the wreck's name *"Carrie Lee"* on her stern.

GAMMA

The *Gamma* is a steel freighter now resting on the shoreline between Georgetown and Seven Mile Beach. This wreck can be explored or at least observed by even a tourist walking down the beach. In 1980, the *Gamma* ran aground on an offshore reef during a storm or Norwester as the Caymanians commonly refer to them. The ship's owners apparently didn't feel that she was worth salvaging and left her to rest on the reef. Sometime later, after another storm, the ship was forced up onto the beach which is where she rests today. Her owners finally decided to hire a salvage company to remove any existing precious metals off of the rusting hull. Thus, all of her brass portholes and fittings are now gone. These pieces were brought to the United States and sold as scrap metal. Although the *Gamma* is not deep enough to dive, snorkelers swimming in the area can enjoy a nice

The *Gamma* was forced up onto the beach by a storm, which is where she rests today. Photo by Daniel Berg.

assortment of fish. Some of the local inhabitants we saw included trunk fish, blue tangs, peacock flounder, parrot fish, rock beauties, and the ever delightful angel fish. The *Gamma* is also a great spot for a photo back drop on the beach, especially if you wait for a Caribbean sunset to enhance the background.

KIRK PRIDE

A visit to the wreck of the *Kirk Pride* is definitely the highlight of any wreck diver's trip to Grand Cayman. The *Kirk Pride* was a 170 foot cargo vessel weighing 498 gross tons. In 1976 the *Kirk Pride* was docked in Georgetown due to engine trouble. A Northeaster was building up, and, in an effort to save the ship from being banged up at dock, it was decided to move her to deeper waters where it was thought she would be much safer. The ship's engines were started, and she was backed out from dock. Unluckily, it was necessary to turn her engines back off in order to switch into forward gear. It was at this time that fate struck. The engines would not start again, and the ship was helplessly driven into a reef. The damaged vessel was now in serious trouble as the ocean water quickly began to seep in. In another attempt to save her, she was fitted with pumps and towed into deeper water. While awaiting a calmer sea that would allow more extensive repairs, the *Kirk Pride* was left anchored in 60 feet of water with drainage pumps running. During the night, the wind changed direction causing the ship to swing around and hover defenseless over the Cayman

75

Bow of the *Kirk Pride* now resting in 800 feet of water. This photograph shows the extensive damage responsible for the ships demise. Also notice that her anchor chain is wrapped completely around her hull, indicating that the ship rolled over at least once while she sunk. Photo by Courtney Platt © 1989.

Stern photo shows a small pinnacle that wedged the *Kirk Pride* into her final resting place. RSL's Pc-1203 submersible which helped to illuminate her stern, can be seen on the right side of the photo. Photo by Courtney Platt © 1989.

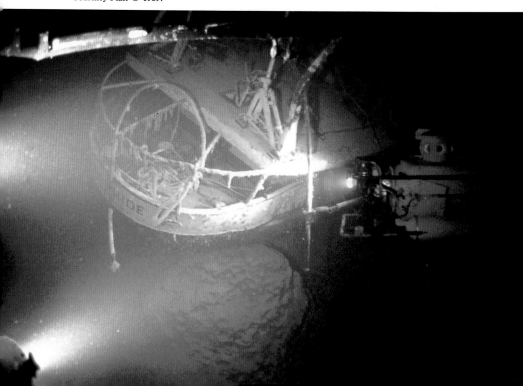

This remarkable overall view taken with only ambient light shows the entire 170 foot long wreck. Courtesy Courtney Platt © 1989.

wall which drops down into 3,000 feet of water. By morning, the pumps had been overcome with sea water, and her two cargo holds were filled. At 9:30 AM January 9, 1976, the ocean once again held an empty surface as the *Kirk Pride* plunged down into unknown depths.

It was not until 1985 that the *Kirk Pride* was rediscovered. While on one of their underwater expeditions, Research Submersibles Ltd. came upon the *Kirk Pride*. She had not fallen into the depth of 3000 feet as it was believed but instead became wedged into her final resting place by two huge pinnacles in 800 feet of water. A small pinnacle or haystack trapped the stern, while a large 60 foot high boulder trapped the bow.

Today, this wreck is far beyond the limits of a sport diver but can be viewed through the use of Research Submersibles Ltd.'s two passenger submersible. The submarine ride will last for about one hour and 30 minutes. This once in a lifetime adventure of dropping to the great depths of the sea and viewing the wreck of the *Kirk Pride* is a memory that will be long lived in anyone's mind.

The wreck is clearly visible and still sits upright. Her name can easily be read on the stern as well as on the bow. She has two cargo compartments. The aft hold still contains a Volkswagen Thing and some sacks of cement.

Portholes, cage lamps, the ship's telegraph, a spare anchor, and a deck winch were all pointed out to us by the operator of the sub.

In November of 1988, National Geographic published a remarkable stern photo that captured almost the entire wreck in one image. To get the photo, two submersibles were used along with two glass floats each filled with four dozen flashbulbs. The combined flash and lights were over five times the intensity of a standard Coast Guard lighthouse. It was one of the most powerful photo flashes ever taken underwater.

Don't be worried, decent photos of the wreck can be taken by anyone using a high speed film such as 400 or 1,000 ASA or video. They will not show the entire wreck in one photo but will document your dive. The entire experience was a perfect way to wrap up a great week of diving on Grand Cayman's shipwrecks.

ORO VERDE

As we found out on our trip, the *Oro Verde* is by far the most popular wreck dive in Grand Cayman. Dive boats run trips to this wreck regularly, day and night.

The *Oro Verde* was an 84 foot, steel cargo vessel which was towed and sunk on May 31, 1980, by the Caymanian government. This was done in a joint effort with dive operators. When the ship was originally sunk, she was completely intact and lay on her starboard side. Today, years later, much of her upper structure has given into the elements of time and collapsed. Her bow section is slightly tilted towards her starboard side, and the deck winch and hand railings are still in place.

If divers enter the wreck through the large square deck hatch, a penetration can be made of about 25 feet forward. Once inside, there are a group of porthole openings you can look through or some inner rooms that are still intact that can be explored.

Behind the bow section of the wreck, divers can swim in and around huge steel plates or just have fun feeding the fish. Be careful not to be too surprised if while feeding the fish, all of a sudden a 300 pound jew fish is right under you waiting for a handout. This jew fish is more commonly referred to as "Sweet Lips" or "George", and has made the wreck of the *Oro Verde* his home. Other inhabitants of the *Oro Verde* include a four foot spotted moray eel that lives in a pipe just forward of the pilot house, a six foot green moray named Kermit who can usually be found under some of the steel plates and a four foot barracuda named Puff. If you look

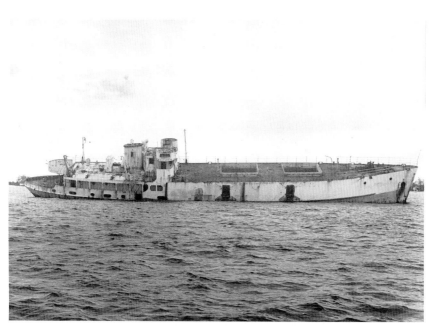

The *Oro Verde* was an 84 foot, steel cargo vessel which was towed and sunk on May 31, 1980 by the Caymanian government. Photo courtesy Caymanian Compass Newspaper.

The *Oro Verde* plunges bow first into 50 feet of water. Photo by Nancy Sefton.

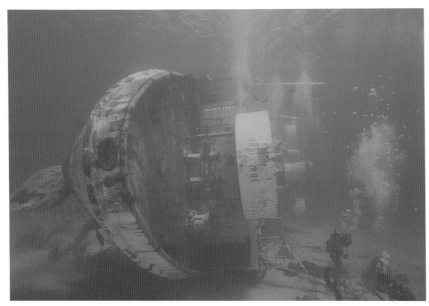

This stern photo was taken immediately after the sinking. Since the photo was taken this area has been broken down by the effects of passing hurricanes. Photo courtesy Nancy Sefton.

The *Oro Verde's* bow rests on its starboard side. Photo by Jozef Koppelman.

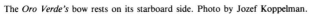

Rick Schwarz holding an eight pound lobster which was later released, in the stern of the Oro Verde. In Grand Cayman lobsters can be taken only in season and not while using SCUBA. Photo by Daniel Berg.

"Sweet Lips", a 300 pound jew fish has made this wreck his home. Photo by Daniel Berg.

hard enough as we did, you may also find a large rock lobster living under the wreck. Due to the constant hand feedings from divers, the most common fish of all are overly plump yellow tail snappers, and some beautiful large angle fish.

Since this wreck lies in 50 feet of water, there is more than sufficient bottom time for exploration and photography. Divers of all experience levels can enjoy the wreck of the *Oro Verde*.

PALACE WRECK

The *Palace Wreck* is the remains of a Norwegian steel hulled brigantine that was forced onto a reef during a storm in 1903. The wreckage is in very shallow water of about eight to ten feet. She is in very small pieces that provide a home for almost every sort of fish and invertebrate represented on the island. Some fish commonly observed here include puffer fish, scorpion fish, flying gurnards, stingrays, parrot fish, and juvenile lobsters. Much of the old rusting hulk remains above the water line, which makes her easy to locate as a beach dive. The *Palace* is an excellent site for snorkelers to explore. According to photographers Courtney and Cozy Platt, "a word of caution should be extended to the explorer of this wreck. When a large surf breaks over this barrier reef, the build-up of water inside the reef sets up a strong current flowing toward the nearest channel in the reef". Divers should avoid these channels when the surf is up. This site is also in an area heavily used by pleasure craft; as always a dive flag is mandatory. Offshore of the wreck is a reef named Palace Wall after this once fine vessel.

RIDGEFIELD

The *Ridgefield* was a Liberian freighter, 441 feet long, 57 feet wide, weighed 7,217 gross tons, and was built at the New England Ship Building Corporation, Portland, Maine in 1943. The *Ridgefield* was originally built as a liberty ship for WW II and christened the *James A. Butts*. In 1947 she was renamed *Lone Star State*, in 1955, *Anniston* and in 1957, *Caldwell*. Later in 1958 she was again sold and renamed *Ridgefield*. On December 18, 1962, while en route from Maracaibo to Galvestone with a cargo of grain and beer, the *Ridgefield* ran aground and broke in two.

Today, the *Ridgefield* is located off the east end of the island in 20 feet of water. Her bow and stern sections are mostly flattened out, a testament to the constant pounding of the ocean waves and power of seasonal tropical storms. Her center section is still standing high and dry above a site that is beautiful to dive or snorkel on.

Rare photograph of the *Ridgefield*.
Courtesy Bill Holtgren collection.

The 593 foot long, 75 foot wide, Costa Cruise Lines luxury cruise ship *Bianca C.* Photo courtesy Steamship Historical Society Collection, University of Baltimore Library.

The *Bianca C* engulfed in flames before sinking off the island of Grenada. Photo by Bettmann Newsphotos, UPI.

GRENADA   British Windward Islands

When the name Grenada is mentioned in conversation, almost everyone associates the island with the U.S. military intervention of 1983. This will soon change, for divers anyway, as wreck divers learn about and spread the word of the *Bianca C*, the largest wreck in the Caribbean. We predict and in fact have already seen the start of a surge of experienced wreck divers traveling to Grenada with only one thing in mind, to dive the *Bianca C*. Grenada does have other interesting attractions for tourists including some magnificent waterfalls, reef dives, good hotels and an abundance of marine life, but the one thing that will always set it apart from other Caribbean islands for divers is the *Bianca C*.

BIANCA C

The *Bianca C* is also known as the *Titanic*, or *Andrea Doria of the Caribbean*. She was a 593 foot long by 75 foot wide, 18,427 ton, Costa Cruise Lines luxury cruise ship owned by the Linea "C" Company of Genoa. Today, she is resting on the ocean floor off the southwest coast of Grenada. The *Bianca C* was built in 1944 by Provencale de Constructions Navales, La Ciotat in yard #161. She had triple screws and 31,500 BHP sulzer diesels that could push her at speeds of up to twenty two knots, two masts and one funnel. She was originaly launched as the *Marechal Petain*, then renamed in 1946 the *La Marseillaise*, and in 1958 she was sold to the Arosa Line Inc. and renamed the *Arosa Sky*. The vessel had accommodations for 200 first class passengers and 1,030 tourist class passengers. The first class dining salon had a glass roofed hall two decks in height. She was also equipped with a swimming pool, solarium, beauty parlor, library, gym, and a children's playground.

The *Bianca C* was sunk once before her construction was ever completed. After being launched in 1944, the *Marechal Petain's* hull was towed to Port Bouc. In August of the same year, the Germans sank the incomplete vessel as they retreated from Southern France. The ship was later raised and completed.

On October 22, 1961, ten days after she left Italy the *Bianca C* was on her last port of call before returning to Europe on her usual run from Naples to La Guaira in Venezuela. She was under the command of Captain Francisco Gravato and at anchor off St. Georges, Grenada when suddenly, before dawn one of her massive boilers exploded instantly killing one of her crewmen. Fuelled by bunker oil in the storage tanks, flames rapidly spread from the engine room to every deck. The explosion on the ship was

85

so massive it sent tremors through the town of St. George. Fortunately for the 750 passengers on board, the people of St. George were awakened and rushed to the fiery scene with a flotilla of 30 small crafts to ferry eveyone to safety. Two crew members were reported dead from burns in the tragedy. Eight crew men including Rodizza Napale, her chief engineer, were treated at a hospital for injuries.

After the initial explosion and subsequent fires, the *Bianca C* was doomed. The island did not possess any marine fire fighting equipment that would have been needed in a salvage attempt of this enormous magnitude. Captain Gravato circled the burning vessel with twenty of his officers trying to direct hopeless fire fighting efforts from a small boat, but ultimately ended up watching this once beautiful vessel destruct before their eyes. On October 24, two days after her initial explosion while the *Bianca C* was still ablaze and beginning to sink, the *H.M.S. Londonderry*, a British frigate, succeeded in securing a cable to the still burning cruise ship. This was no easy feat as a crew from the *Londonderry* had to face burning deck plates and billows of steam in order to fasten the tow line. The *Londonderry* then attempted to beach the *Bianca C* in a spot where she would not be blocking the harbor, but after towing her a few miles through strong currents and winds, her burnt hull plates gave out and she went down off Port Saline.

In gratitude for the efforts of the Grenadian people, the Italian government sent a statue of "Jesus of the Sea", which can now be seen guarding the harbor at St. George's.

The *Bianca C* now rests only one mile from shore which is about a fifteen minute boat ride. Although she sits in 160 feet of water leaning slightly to her starboard side, divers can reach her deck hand railings at 95 feet and cover most of her decks without descending lower than 120 feet. Water temperature here is usually a steady 80 degrees, and the visibility on and around the wreck is usually better than 50 feet. The current over the wreck is very powerful; divers have to pull themselves down the dive boat's anchor line, hand over hand, to keep from drifting away. This deep but interesting shipwreck is only for very experienced divers due to the strong currents and depth. As an extra note of caution all divers should be conservative on their dive schedule since the nearest recompression chamber is on the island of Barbados. The area is inhabited by all sorts of marine life including some huge eagle rays, turtles, and barracuda. The *Bianca C* has not been visited by too many divers, but those who have had the privilege of exploring this enormous wreck will surely remember her as one of their most interesting dives.

In February of 1989, a group of experienced wreck divers from Long Island,

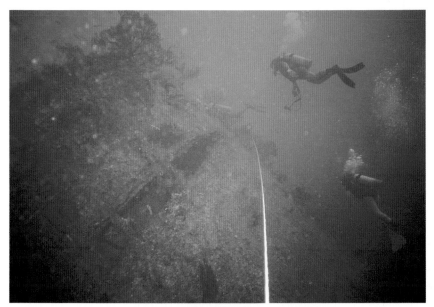

Divers explore the fire gutted remains of the *Bianca C*. Photo courtesy Herb Segars.

Stern mast of the *Bianca C*. Photo
courtesy Rick Schwarz.

Hank Garvin (left) and Chris Dillon displaying the ships bell they recovered from the *Bianca C* during their 1989 expedition. Photo courtesy Rick Schwarz.

Ships bell carefully cleaned enough to read "M/N *Bianca C*, Genova". Photo by Daniel Berg.

New York comprised of Chris Dillon, Hank Garvin & Rick Schwarz travelled to Grenada, dove the *Bianca C* and recovered her bell. Despite other contradictory reports this group noted that the condition of the wreck has deteriorated extensively. Since much of her brass portholes and fixtures are missing it can be concluded that the *Bianca C* may have already been commercially salvaged for her valuable brass, and due to natural causes of saltwater the structure of the ship has become very weak. This could also have been caused by extensive fire damage incurred before her sinking. The group was also able to find their way into the ship's china room, and brought up some beautiful third class china which will be displayed on the island of Grenada as well as in the United States in order to promote diving on this beautiful Caribbean island.

BUCCANEER

The *Buccaneer* was a coastal schooner, which was scuttled, back in 1978, to form a fish haven and dive site. The *Buccaneer*, which is sitting in 80 feet of water, has done both magnificently, her hull supports a wide array of tropical fish and she is visited by hundreds of divers each year. Because her structure has become beautifully encrusted with soft corals and sponges, divers have found this site to be excellent for photography. The *Buccaneer* is also an ideal warm up dive for the deep wreck of the *Bianca C*.

GUANAJA   Bay Islands, Honduras

Guanaja is the second largest of the Bay Islands of Honduras. Guanaja is a beautiful island with a combination of jungle, pine forest, and sea.

As well as some interesting wrecks there are many colorful shallow dives that can be done in tranquility without the worry of currents or surge making the island especially convenient for the novice diver.

DONNA M

The *Donna M* was sunk by George Cundiff, owner of a local dive operation and hotel, as a fish haven and dive location in July of 1986. This 85 foot long shrimp boat now rests on a sandy bottom in 80 feet of water, just inside of a barrier reef.

According to George, billions of silver sides have made this wreck their home. Visibility at this site is anywhere between 50 and 100 feet.

GEORGE'S WRECK

This huge steamer, which is approximately 350 feet long, was sunk at George's Key in the 1920's. She now rests on a coral bed with her remains scattered over a large area. Since she sits in only 12 feet of water outside of a reef, divers and snorkelers can also enjoy swimming around this site.

Things to be seen in the wreckage include the ship's boilers, plates and shafts. Visibility here has been reported to be anywhere from 75 to 200 feet.

JADO TRADER

The *Jado Trader* was sunk in 1987 in order to form an artificial fish haven. This 260 foot long freighter, which was converted into a refrigerator ship, now rests on a sandy bottom, completely intact, in 105 feet of water. Before the town finally decided to have the *Jado Trader* sunk, she sat in the harbor rusting for five to six years. George Cundiff took the task of sinking the vessel next to Mile Deep Wall. The wreck lies on her starboard side with her bow facing the wall. Visibility here ranges from 80 to over 200 feet.

The *Jado Trader,* a 260 foot long freighter sunk in 1987. Photo courtesy George Condiff.

Jado Trader, Photo courtesy
George Condiff.

Although the wreck has not yet fully developed into a reef, she has attracted a good amount of fish and is starting to become covered with coral, sponge, and other marine life. Some of the fish to be seen include silver sides, large grouper, jew fish, and spiny oysters.

Close to the wreck lie two huge coral pinnacles. One of these formations has a volcanic cave inside. They both come to within 20 feet of the surface.

Divers will not want to forget their cameras for this site. To say the least, this abandoned freighter turned reef is very photogenic.

MYSTERY WRECK

The *Mystery Wreck*, also known as *No Name Wreck*, is a steel hulled vessel about 90 feet in length and is of unknown origin. Somehow she sunk and now rests upside down on a sandy bottom. This wreck lies 50 yards from a coral finger in a depth of 42 feet.

Divers can penetrate the stern of the ship which sticks into the mud, but should they venture inside, they may have to share it with a huge grouper, estimated to weigh almost 1,000 pounds, who has chosen to make this wreck his home.

RUTHIE C

The *Ruthie C* is a 65 foot long vessel which sits in 42 feet of water, directly in front of the Plaza Del Sol Hotel. She was sunk by the hotel owner, George Condiff, in May of 1986 as a dive site. The wreck is now sitting at the base of a wall on a sand and grass bottom. Visibility ranges from 30 to about 70 feet.

JAMAICA   Western Caribbean

Jamaica is the third largest island in the Caribbean. This beautiful island is made up of plains, mangrove swamps, rivers that flow through the mountains, and a tropical rain forest.

Although we have not found too many wreck sites being used by sport divers in Jamaica, the island is full of coral formations, caverns and overhangs for divers to explore. Jamaica does have many more wrecks and as more divers travel to the island, these will be found, explored and enjoyed.

ANN BONNIE

Although the wreck of the *Ann Bonnie* is not the remains of a historical shipwreck, it is a good wreck for newly certified or resort course divers. The 50 foot long wreck is actually a boat sunk by a local resort, and has been modified to look like an old pirate ship. The *Ann Bonnie* even has cannons mounted to her decks. Granted they are concrete reproductions but their presence still gives divers a nice photo opportunity. The *Ann Bonnie* is in 30 feet of water and visibility on the site is best described as crystal clear. For information on a trip to this wreck contact the Club Caribbean or Jamaica Jamaica.

CAYMAN TRADER

This old freighter was abandoned and left rusting in the harbor before the Harbor Master scuttled her in 1980. She can now be found resting between South Key and South East Key in Kingston Harbor. This site must be dove on a calm day and unless you are familiar with the area it is a hard wreck to find. Depth at the site ranges from 60 to 70 feet and visibility has been described as murky.

LA DOMICANA

La Domicana was a three masted schooner sunk in 1951 by a hurricane. She can now be found inside Kingston Harbor off the old airport runway. Depth on the wreck ranges from 20 to 30 feet and visibility is usually poor, only two to three feet. This dive should only be attempted by advanced divers due to the poor visibility and the amount of nets and monofilament fishing lines that cover the wreck, creating possible snags.

PLANES

The remains of two small *Cessna* aircraft can be found off the western tip of Jamaica in Negril. The *Planes* were abandoned and had been left sitting at the Negril Airport. After hurricane Gilbert roared through the area both planes were damaged beyond repair. In December of 1988, a local dive operation sunk the wreckage. One *Cessna* can be found intact at a depth of 50 feet on a sand bottom just next to a reef. The second *Cessna* is now resting in 90 feet of water.

TEXAS

The *Texas* was a British Mine Layer which was sunk by collision in 1942.

The 100 foot long wreck is now sitting upright in South Kingston Channel. Divers will reach her smoke stack in 80 feet and her propeller in 110 feet of water. Divers will also find an anti-aircraft gun still mounted on her forward deck. The area has no noticeable current, but is located inside the shipping lanes. Anyone who would like to visit this site would have to rent a boat from Port Royal and check with the harbor master for a shipping forecast. According to Peter Espeut, diving officer for W.I. University, the exact location of the wreck can be obtained from the University of the West Indies Sub Aqua Club by contacting the zoology department.

LITTLE CAYMAN   Cayman Islands

The smallest of the Cayman Islands, Little Cayman is only ten square miles in size. The island has only a hand full of residents and is probably best known for the exciting sport fishing found here. This quiet island in the sun with its pink sand beaches is perfect for getting away from civilization. The diving here is as beautiful as in its sister islands.

SOTO TRADER

The *Soto Trader* was a 120 foot long by 30 foot wide, steel hulled island freighter registered in Grand Cayman. In April of 1975, she was en route from Grand Cayman to Cayman Brac, carrying a cargo of beer, gasoline, diesel fuel, cement mixers, and a jeep and stopped at Little Cayman only to off load diesel for local generators on the island. While at anchor in an area called The Flats, her crew was pumping diesel fuel into 55 gallon drums which would later be transported by small boats to the island when tragedy struck. Some of the diesel had leaked onto her decks and ignited from a spark, quickly engulfing the vessel in flames. One crew member died of burns almost immediately, while another lived through being transported to a hospital on Cayman Brac only to pass away two hours later. The rest of her crew eluded injury. The *Soto Trader* burned from 3:00 PM until 7:00 AM the next day before slipping beneath the waves to her watery grave.

The wreck is now sitting in 60 feet of water on the southwest side of Little Cayman, completely intact and upright. According to Gary Moore, a veteran Caribbean diver, and Croy McCoy, an island dive guide, divers will find three large cargo doors on her main deck, all open, which allow for easy access to her cargo holds. Inside her holds are some remains of her cargo including the jeep chassis and cement mixers. There is a crane mounted midships with the boom facing bow to stern. A big green moray eel can usually be found

Bow of the 120 foot long, 30 foot wide, steel hulled island freighter *Soto Trader*. Photo courtesy Nancy Sefton.

Soto Trader's stern. Photo by Gary Moore.

living inside the boom. The wreck's pilot house is still intact, and her rudder and propeller can be seen sitting just on top of a coral reef. The area is frequently visited by eagle rays, puffer fish, shrimp, and angel fish. This site is not dove too often. Unfortunately, the *Soto Trader* is situated on the opposite side of the island from where all of the popular reef dives are. If, however, you can schedule a dive here, we think you will be quite pleased. Expected visibility ranges from 40 to 70 feet.

MARTINIQUE   French West Indies

The shipwrecks on this island are quite distinct from any other Caribbean island. Not many people know about what we refer to as *"The Truck Lagoon of the Caribbean"*. This area contains at least eighteen shipwrecks, most of which were sunk on the same day. This tragedy sounds bad enough considering that on most all hands went down with their ships, but this was nothing compared to the destruction ashore. The cause behind this catastrophe was the eruption of Mount Pele's volcano. The date was May 8, 1902. The New York Times reported that over 40,000 people were killed when the entire cap of the volcano was blown off, followed by a down pour of molten lava. Captain Whatter of the vessel *Roddam*, the only ship in the harbor to stay afloat, reported that he was talking to Joseph Plissono, who was in a boat alongside, when he saw a tremendous cloud of smoke and cinders rushing with terrific rapidity over the town and port, completely and instantly enveloping all in a sheet of flame and raining fire. The suddenness of this calamity which did not even permit ships at anchor in the Harbor of St. Pierre to make sail and escape is almost incomprehensible.

Today, Martinique is a quiet, lush, tropical island enjoyed mostly by French tourists. On land there are still many reminders of the tragedy, but many have forgotten about the vessels lost in St. Pierre Bay. The following is information on wrecks that have been found and have become dive sites. Water temperature on Martinique is generally a constant 80 degrees; visibility ranges from 80 to 100 feet, but is sometimes reduced drastically due to the fine volcanic silt that covers the sea bed.

CLEMENTINA

The wreck of the vessel *Clementina* is resting in deep water of over 160 feet. She sits on a flat sand bottom totally covered with volcanic ash.

DIAMANT

The *Diamant* is a wood hulled tug boat resting on her side in 100 to 115

Wood hulled tug boat *Diamant.* Photo by Mason Logie.

feet of water. Her remains are partly deteriorated but her engine and boilers can easily be recognized. The *Diamant* was towing a barge at the time of the eruption, so close by lies the Barge wreck, but it is not intact.

GABRIELLE

All that is known of this ship is that she was once a wooden, three masted sailboat. She was riding at anchor with her cargo holds empty at the time of the eruption. According to Georges Marie Sainte, the *Gabrielle's* second officer, the force of the explosion quickly dismasted and capsized her. Five of her crew were rescued, but all of their hair and clothes were burned off.

The *Gabrielle* now rests on a sand bottom in 100 to 115 feet of water. Divers report that pieces of exquisite china and human bones are still being found in the wreckage.

GIALLIA

The *Giallia* is the only wreck in the bay that was not sunk during the 1902 eruption. She was a dredge boat that while doing work around St. Pierre dock in 1930, sunk. She now lies in 100 feet of water and is fairly intact.

GRAPPLER

The *Grappler* was a 860 ton cable repair steamer belonging to the West India and Panama Telegraph Company of London. According to the New York Times, she was one of the first ships to disappear after the eruption. The *Grappler* was lost with all hands aboard. She is now resting in approximately 105 feet of water.

ITALIAN YACHT

The wreck of the *Italian Yacht* lies on a sloped bottom. Mason Logie, owner of Dive Away Inc., a New York based company that specializes in exotic wreck diving, says that her bow is in 65 feet and her stern is in 130 feet of water. Since her sinking, the wreck has deteriorated and has begun to break up.

NORTH AMERICAN

The wood remains of the vessel *North American* lie on a ledge in more than 160 feet of water. The ship is broken up and has also begun to deteriorate.

RAISINIER

The *Raisinier* is one of the shallowest wrecks in the bay, sitting in only 50 feet of water. According to John Fine's article on "Mont Pele's Underwater Graveyard" this wreck is very photogenic. Divers can sometimes still find brass pins, but the wreck has already been picked pretty clean.

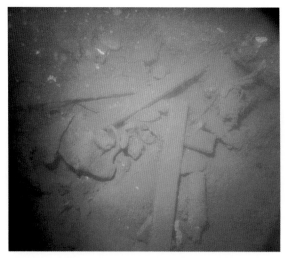

Debris inside the *Italian Yacht*. Look closely at the photograph and you will notice a boot, bottle and china cup. Photo by Mason Logie.

RORAIMA

The *Roraima* was a steal hulled Quebec Line steamship, and is the largest wreck in the bay. She was transporting a cargo of potassium when the eruption occurred. Her combustible cargo caught fire, and she burned for three days before sinking.

Her burnt remains are now sitting upright with a slight tilt to her port side. She sits on a sloping bottom where her depth ranges from 160 to 205 feet. The *Roraima* is mostly intact except for her bow which has broken down and her stern which has split from the main wreckage.

Quebec Line Steamship *Roraima.* Photo courtesy Steamship Historical Society Collection, University of Baltimore Library.

The *Roraima,* the day after the volcano erupted in flames before sinking. Courtesy Steve Bielenda collection.

Drawing of the *Roraima* as she rests today. Courtesy Steve Bielenda.

TAMAYA

The *Tamaya* was a 566 ton, three masted iron bark, built in Liverpool in 1862 and owned by Rozier and Nantes. Sunk with all hands, the *Tamaya* is now a deep wreck, resting on her starboard side in 260 feet of water which makes her to deep for sport divers to explore.

TERESA LO VICO

The *Teresa Lo Vico* was a two masted sailing vessel, weighing 585 tons built in 1874. At the time of the eruption, she was carrying a cargo of building supplies that included tiles, rope, and cement in barrels. When diving on this fairly intact, large wooden wreck, divers will see tiles stacked on her deck, rope still coiled, and the now hardened cement cargo which has taken the form of the wood barrels, now disintegrated, that were once used for transportation. Three of the *Teresa Lo Vicos* crew survived the eruption and sinking. Jean Louis, a mechanic, reported that the ship was moored at the foot of Rue d'Orange, only 150 feet offshore. "At 8:00 AM an enormous mass of the crater detached and was hurled toward the city". Jean Louis managed to abandon his sinking ship and, with the use of a small canoe he found adrift, rescued 11 sailors from the Bay.

The *Teresa Lo Vico* now lies on a sloping bottom with depths ranging from 100 to 120 feet of water.

The *Teresa Lo Vico* was carrying a cargo of cement in wood barrels. Although the Barrels have disintegrated divers can still see the now hardened cement which has taken the form of the original wood barrels. Photo by Mason Logie.

Divers will also find neatly wrapped coils of rope amongst the wreckage of the *Teresa Lo Vico*. Photo by Mason Logie.

PUERTO RICO

Eastern Caribbean

The mountainous island of Puerto Rico is like a visit into history. Tourists can visit El Morro Castle, a massive fortress built by the Spanish in 1510, 400 year old churches, or the San Juan Gate, the only remaining gate from a wall which dates back to the early 1500's built around San Juan.

Diving in Puerto Rico has never been highly publicized but could compare with almost any tropical island. Most dive sites are located offshore where water clarity is crystal clear. The water close to the island tends to be a little murky due to rain run off. Most of the more popular dive sights are reef dives. These sights are heavily populated with squirrelfish, spadefish, eagle rays, morays, groupers, and the occasional nurse shark. Many historic shipwrecks are still hidden in the shallow water surrounding Puerto Rico, some are reported to be treasure ships, others slave and cargo vessels. The list of wrecks within this text is sure to grow as more divers investigate, search and find shipwrecks in Puerto Rico.

AIRPLANE

The *Airplane* wreck is the remains of a six passenger *Piper Cherokee* monoplane. The *Piper*, which was built in Lock Haven, Pennsylvania, is now resting in 50 feet of water. Much of the aircraft is covered by sponge and coral.

DESTROYER

James Abbot, who charters dives in Puerto Rico, says that there is an old navy destroyer sunk off the east end of Vieques Island. The ship was apparently once used for target practice and is now very broken up and scattered in 35 to 40 feet of water. The *Destroyer* wreck is resting on a sandy bottom and holds a good amount of marine life.

TUG BOAT

This wreck is an 80 foot long, ocean going tug that ran aground on Culebrita Reef. The wreck is sitting upright and intact in very shallow water of only 40 feet. Coral, sponge and a good assortment of marine creatures can be found all over this site.

BARGE

An old sugar cane barge of unknown origin lies about one mile off the shore of Cayo Santiago off Humacao. This wreck lies intact and upright in forty feet of water on a sand and grass bottom.

The marine life here has been reported to be average, and there is usually no current to hinder divers.

ROATAN **Bay Islands, Hondoras**

Roatan is the largest of the Bay Islands and the most developed. Located approximately 900 miles south-southwest of Florida, this island is about 32 miles long by two miles wide.

Diving in Roatan is similar to that of Guanaja. There are also caverns, caves, cliffs, and crevices to be explored.

GWENDOLYN

The *Gwendolyn* was a 200 foot long, Honduran mine sweeper. She ran into an offshore reef on the northwest side of Roatan in 1955 and quickly sank to the bottom. She is now lying upside down on the ocean floor in 120 feet of water. Visibility on this wreck ranges from 20 to 50 feet.

PRINCE ALBERT

Off the south side of Roatan lies the wreck of the *Prince Albert*. This 140 foot long, steel hulled island freighter had exhausted her useful life and sat unattended and rusting for quite some time. She was finally donated by the owner, a Roatan business man, to be sunk as an artificial reef.

In preparation for her sinking, The *Prince Albert's* hatches were removed and several four foot by six foot holes were cut through her bulkheads. These steps assured easy and safe diver exploration of the ship's interior. The *Prince Albert* was then taken in tow by the shrimp boat *Sheena Mc*. While under tow, the freighter became unmanageable and ran aground on a reef where she remained for over a week, refusing to budge and actually snapping the tow cable of the stuggling shrimp boat. The trawler *Lady Eleanor* and her volunteer crew with the benefit of favorable weather conditions were finally able to pull the *Prince Albert* off the reef and towed the ship to her present location. The crew opened her valves, and within an hour and a half she sunk to the bottom.

The wreck now sits upright and intact in 65 feet of water in a sand channel.

The *Prince Albert,* a 140 foot long steel hulled island freighter had exhausted her useful life and sat unattended for a few years. Photo courtesy Co Co View Resort.

The *Prince Albert* was taken in tow by the shrimp boat Sheena Mc. Photo courtesy Co Co View Resort.

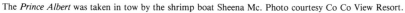

She seemingly invites divers to explore her pilot house, passageways, cargo holds, and compartments. Visibility at the site changes with the tides, ranging from excellent to a little murky.

Within the next few years this wreck is going to develop into a stunning reef supporting an eco chain that ranges from plant life to large predators.

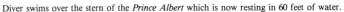

Diver swims over the stern of the *Prince Albert* which is now resting in 60 feet of water.

The upside down remains of the *Barge* wreck. A crane which had once been mounted atop the barges deck now sticks out from under the wreckage. Photo by Daniel Berg.

ST. CROIX   U.S. Virgin Islands

St. Croix is the largest of the U.S. Virgin Islands. The island is 22 miles long, six miles wide and is located 40 miles south of St. Thomas. The diving here is great and was recently improved by the sinking of three ships on the west side of the island.

BARGE

This wreck lies just outside of Christiansted Harbor. Although the history behind the sinking of this barge is unknown, we believe she was sunk as a fish haven. Her remains which begin at 75 feet and slope down to over 95 feet of water do make for an interesting dive. The wreckage also includes a crane that had been mounted atop the main deck. This has now broken off and sticks out from under the *Barge's* hull. The wreck which lies upside down is usually explored and sometimes photographed before divers move on to observe the coral reefs in the surrounding area.

MODEL A TRUCK

Not exactly your typical wreck, this old truck is an interesting dive anyway. The *Model A* sits in 130 feet of water just east of Christiansted Harbor in an area called Scotch Banks. The truck is reported to have fallen off a ship in the 1950's. Today, she is an absolutely magnificent little wreck to dive on, covered with sponges and black coral, and usually a gray angle fish or two can be seen swimming in and around her.

NORTHWIND

The *Northwind* is a 75 foot long, steel hulled ocean tug named after Mel Fisher's salvage boat that was used on the *Atocha* treasure recovery. According to Tom Long, the tug was used as a prop for the movie "Dreams of Gold", starring Loretta Swit and Cliff Robertson a story about Fisher's search for the *Atocha*. After filming was completed, the tug was left behind. The *Northwind* was sunk by Cruzan Divers Inc. and Ship Services in May of 1986.

Today, the vessel sits upright in 55 feet of water. Average visibility in the area ranges from 100 to 200 feet, and divers will marvel at the abundance of marine life which includes goat fish, rays, yellow tails, and an occasional turtle.

Named after Mel Fisher's salvage vessel for the movie "Dreams of Gold" this tug is now known as the *Northwind*. Photo by Doug Perrine.

A skate swims over the remains of a small Cessna airplane. Photo by Daniel Berg.

PLANE

This is definitely the smallest wreck off the island of St. Croix. Jimmy Antoine, a local dive operator, explained that in 1978 this little two seated *Cessna* ran out of gas and crashed into the sea. Unfortunately, her pilot did not survive the crash. The *Plane* is very broken up in 22 feet of water, and divers have to use their imagination to recognize any of her parts. On the day we dove this site, an octopus and several skates were found in the sand around the wreck.

ROSAOMAIRA

The *Rosaomaira* is a 177 foot long, steel hulled Venezuelan freighter. She capsized while her cargo was being prepared for off loading. Apparently the weight of her cargo was not balanced correctly, causing the ship to tip. After attempting to right the vessel and failing, it was discovered that the ship's owner was trying to smuggle diesel fuel onboard. The *Rosaomaira* was then towed to Butler Bay and sunk in April of 1986 with the aid of explosives.

This wreck, known also as the *Rosa*, is now sitting in 110 feet of water, completely intact and upright. Left untouched since her sinking, her crews

Bow with still legible lettering reading *Rosaomaira*. This 177 foot long freighter was sunk in April, 1986. Photo by Doug Perrine.

At *Truck Lagoon,* located just west of the *Northwind* wreck divers will find the remains of five old Hess oil trucks. Photo by Doug Perrine.

clothing and personal effects can still be found in their cabins. Average visibility ranges from 80 to 200 feet, and there is usually little or no current.

SUFFOLK MAID

Only a few hundred yards south of the *Rosaomaira* and a hundred yards north of the *Northwind* lies the wreck of the *Suffolk Maid*. She was a 144 foot long, steel hulled North sea trawler. The *Suffolk Maid* was washed up onto Frederiksted Pier during a hurricane in 1984.

In December of 1985, the *Suffolk Maid* was towed to its present location and scuttled. She is know sitting upright on the ocean floor in 60 feet of water. Her superstructure was removed prior to her sinking. Again, this site has little or no current, and visibility is almost always good, ranging from 100 to 200 feet. Divers can still recognize the ship's name on her bow.

TRUCK LAGOON

Truck Lagoon is a site located just west of the *Northwind* tug. Divers will find the remains of five old Hess oil trucks that were transported here to develop an artificial reef. The trucks, which have been on the bottom for about ten years, are on a sloping sand bottom, ranging from 60 to 70 feet of water.

SINT EUSTATIUS   Netherland Antilles

Sint Eustatius is a small island, only four miles long by two miles wide. Aside from the wreck site we have listed, other underwater interests include the occasional sightings of rays and turtles. However, Sint Eustatius is a preserve, so nothing can be brought up from dives; this includes shells, coral and artifacts.

SUPERMARKET

This area not only contains the remains of one sunken vessel, but a conglomeration of at least three and possibly as many as seven different shipwrecks. Spread across the sea floor in 30 feet of water are ballast piles, anchors, cannons, cannon balls, bottles, clay pipes, and possibly even an old musket or two. Local laws prohibit the removal of any artifacts, so remember to look but don't touch. The area also has an abundance of interesting marine creatures that include an occasional turtle.

ST. KITTS   **British Leeward Islands**

St. Kitts was discovered by Christopher Columbus in 1493. The island became an Associated Statehood with England in 1960 and achieved independence in 1983. Topside attraction on the island include Brimstone Hill, an old fort built in the late 1600's. The fortress was the site of a battle between the French and English in 1782. The view from Brimstone Hill Fort is, to say the least, spectacular.

Diving on St. Kitts should be fascinating for divers of all experience levels. The best dive sites are located a mile or so off shore where clear water, big fish, and beautiful coral abound.

CHRISTINA

The *Christina* was a ferry boat that sank on August 1, 1970. According to Kenneth Samuel, owner of a local dive shop, the wreck is now sitting on top of a reef in 80 feet of water. This site offers good to excellent visibility and an exciting assortment of marine life.

LA' AMIGO

The wreck of the *La' Amigo* is located one mile west of the *Taleta* wreck. This vessel was a ferry similar to the *Christina*. She was sunk intentionally in the fall of 1988 as a dive site and is now resting on a coral sea bed in 60 feet of water.

RIVER TOIRE

The *River Toire* was sunk in the late 1970's. She is a huge vessel, approximately 150 feet long by 60 feet wide, and is now sitting on a clean sand bottom. Her mid section is still intact, but her aft port side has given into the elements of time and collapsed.

This wreck is completely covered with sea life. Everything from schooling bait fish to larger predators and crustaceans make this vessel a delight to explore.

TALETA

The *Taleta* was a cargo ship approximately 130 feet long by 50 feet wide that had been left anchored in the harbor, abandoned. One morning in

1986 at about 6:00 AM, she slipped beneath the waves just a quarter mile off Basseterre. This steel vessel is now resting intact in 60 feet of water and is surrounded by a beautiful coral reef. Visibility on this site ranges from 50 to 100 feet but can be a bit on the cloudy side. There is usually a mild current.

ST. LUCIA   **British Windward Islands**

The tropical volcanic island of St. Lucia is located between St. Vincent and Martinique. The island is known for its dramatic walls, drift dives, yellow sea horses, and diverse marine life. In the past, St. Lucia has not been a good wreck diving location. It seems that any ship that had the misfortune of sinking near this island sunk in water much too deep for sport divers, 3,000 feet. Now, this has all changed. The fisheries department has started, and it plans to continue to sink abandoned vessels in shallow water. Today, divers can have the best of both worlds as they can enjoy reef as well as wreck diving on this lush, tropical paradise.

LESLEEN M

The *Lesleen M* was a 165 foot long, steel hulled cargo vessel. Lue Flotte and Mary Ellen Kenny, New York based photographers, report that she

Lesleen M in tow to be sunk as an artificial reef. Photo courtesy Lucien Flotte.

The vessel has now begun to take water onto her main deck. Photo by Lucien Flotte.

Sinking stern first was a dramatic end of this once fine vessel's sailing days. Notice the ship's bell still in place in the bow. Photo by Lucien Flotte.

Finally sinking after a half hour the *Lesleen M* had just begun a new life as a artificial reef. Photo by Lucien Flotte.

Bow of the *Lesleen M.* This photograph was taken immediately after her sinking. Today much of the wreck is encrusted with colorful coral. Photo by Lucien Flotte.

Air still escaping as the ship settles into her final resting place. Photo by Lucien Flotte.

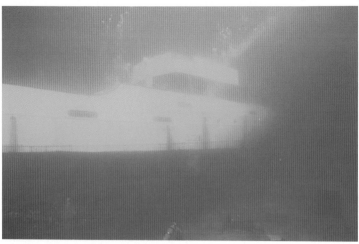

was intentionally sunk in 1986 by the ministry of fisheries with the intention of creating an artificial reef. The *Lesleen M* was prepared for sinking by the St. Lucian Port Authority. They removed her mast and wheel house as these items may have caused the ship to protrude too high off the sea floor, possibly causing a hazard to navigation. The Port Authority also cut holes in the vessel above her water line in order to help the ship sink quickly yet not take on any water while being moved. She was towed by the Port Authority tug to a spot in 90 feet of water, but due to a strong current and a half hour of sinking, she drifted quite a bit and ended up sitting upright in 65 feet of water.

This site already has a good coating of sponges and coral. Angel fish, groupers, tiger groupers, grunts, hogfish, silversides, pipe fish, sergeant majors, jacks, squirrel fish, and large yellow sea horses are only a very small example of the types of fish observed here each dive.

De Havilland Heron, four engine aircraft. Photo courtesy Bruce Cotler collection.

PLANE

The *Plane* wreck is that of an old *De Havilland Heron*, a four engine light transport plane built in Hatfield, England. In 1984, after being found abandoned, she was towed to a sight off the south side of the island and sunk as a dive location. The *Plane* now sits upright, bow facing towards the shore, in 100 feet of water on a sand bottom. Average visibility at the wreck ranges from 40 to 50 feet.

Very close to the *Plane* wreck is the remains of the freighter *Wawinet*.

WAWINET

The *Wawinet* was an abandoned 4,000 ton freighter that had sat in the harbor, unattended for at least two years. She was towed to a spot off the south side of St. Lucia and sunk to form an artificial reef in 1984. The *Wawinet* is now sitting intact in 100 feet of water on a hard packed silt

115

bottom. According to Keith Nichols, a biologist with the Fisheries Department, the area tends to have a strong current and is suitable for experienced divers only.

SINT MAARTEN   Netherland Antilles

Sint Maarten is another small island of the Netherlands Antilles, only 37 square miles in size. Sint Maarten is shared by two states, Sint Maarten and St. Martin. The first is the Dutch side; while the latter is controlled by the French West Indies.

Visibility on the island averages at 120 feet, and the reefs are shallow, starting at 30 feet. Diving on the island is just beginning to become popular. Divers will see a large amount of marine life including corals, sponges, reef fish, rays and barracuda.

H.M.S. PROSELYTE

The *H.M.S. Proselyte* was a 32 gun English frigate. On September 4, 1801, while under the command of Captain George Fowke, the warship hit a reef which now bears her name. This area is also known as Man-of-War Shoal. None of her 215 crew members were lost. It was later determined that the *Proselyte* was lost due to the negligence of her master, L. Williams.

The *Proselyte* is now resting in 50 feet of water off the south side of the island, and is one of Sint Maarten's most popular dive sites. About 20 cannons and three large anchors are still easily recognizable, but many other artifacts such as cannon balls, musket balls, nails, spikes, and pottery can be found by fanning the sand. Beautiful marine life such as parrot fish, angel fish and barracudas can also be found around the wreckage.

ST. VINCENT and the GRENADINES   B.W.I.

Located in the south east Caribbean, over 100 islands and cays make up St. Vincent and the Grenadines. St. Vincent, which is the largest island in the group, is a volcanic island with amazingly steep mountains. It seems as if the entire island is covered with lush tropical vegetation. The beaches on St. Vincent quickly reveal their volcanic origin since they are composed of black sand. Diving here is extraordinary. Divers can visit reefs, caves, wrecks and can enjoy all with excellent visibility. The Grenadines, all located south of St. Vincent, have white sand beaches. Here travelers will find romantic, unspoiled, lush tropical islands waiting to be explored. Diving in the Grenadines is excellent. Hard and soft corals, huge schools of bait fish, drift diving, cave diving, and wall diving are only a small example of the diversified unspoiled waters of the Grenadines.

M.V. LERICO

The *M.V. Lerico*, a freighter approximately 200 feet long, was sunk by the Coast Guard in 1985. This wreck can now be found in 90 feet of water off the Isle A'Quatre, Bequia. She is resting on a sand bottom, and her structure supports a full eco chain of tropical fish. Average visibility in the area is 40 to 60 feet.

LILIANA

The remains of the sailboat *Liliana* are sitting upright in 90 feet of water off Devil's Table, Bequia. She was constructed of ferro cement and sank in the early 1980's.

H.M.S. PURINA

This wreck is unidentified but is thought to be the remains of an English warship. Approximately 100 feet long, she is located off the island of Mayreau. The *H.M.S. Purina*, as the story goes, had been sitting at anchor

H.M.S. Purina, an unidentified wreck sitting in 40 feet of water. Photo courtesy Glenroy Adams.

in the harbor; she pulled anchor and was heading for open water when she ran onto a reef and sank.

Today the wreck is found in 40 feet of water on a sand bottom. Her engines and huge boilers are easily identified. The bow and stern of the wreck are relatively intact, but deterioration elsewhere on the vessel leaves only a skeletal outline of this once fine warship. Glenroy Adams, the only native scuba instructor in the area, tells us that the captain's toilet is the favorite spot on the wreck for divers to take pictures. Glenroy also stated that the *Purina* is covered with marine life and is a truly beautiful dive.

SIEMSTRAD

The *Siemstrad* was an old 120 foot long ferry sunk in the late 1970's. She sits intact on the ocean floor in 85 feet of water and is located inside Kingstown harbor.

ST. THOMAS   U.S. Virgin Islands

St. Thomas is by far the best known of the U.S. Virgin Islands. Excellent shopping, clear water, intimate beaches, night life and of course spectacular diving can all be found here. The reefs off St. Thomas support all types of tropical fish. In fact it's not uncommon for a diver to see parrotfish, damselfish, peacock flounder, turtles, and sting rays all on the same dive.

AIRPLANE

This wreck is that of a *Lockheed Constellation* aircraft that was rumored to be designed by Howard Hughes just after WW II. The cargo plane had four engines and a triple tail. The plane was originally commissioned for the U.S. Air Force, but after many years of service she was purchased to deliver fruits and vegetables between islands. According to Debbie & Joe Vogel, who own and operate a local dive operation, the plane crashed in 1980 while en route between St. Croix and St. Thomas. The accident happened at dusk while a misty rain was present. No radio distress calls were heard; it seemed as though she just plunged into the sea. The *Constellation* stayed together and afloat overnight, allowing survivors to be rescued. Unfortunately, her pilot, co-pilot and one of her crew members were killed in the crash. The following morning the aircraft was in tow tail first, but she sank off Fortuna Bay before she could make it to shore.

The *Airplane* wreckage now sits in 45 feet of water about 100 yards off

Lockhead Constellation aircraft. Photo courtesy Bruce Cotler collection.

shore on the southwest end of the island. She has been scattered a little from the heavy winds of a few hurricanes, but divers will still be able to find two thirds of her fuselage and her wing intact. Her landing gear, a still inflated tire, and even windshield wipers are all recognizable. To give you an idea of the size of this huge aircraft, just imagine a 727 sitting in crystal clear water in only 45 feet of water. Bringing a camera goes without saying for this site.

CARTANSER SENIOR

This 190 foot long, steel hulled freighter has an interesting history. During World War II, she was used to transport goods. After the war, she was used to carry various cargos between islands. She was brought to St. Thomas in 1970 and was abandoned by her captain and crew. By this time, the vessel had definitely seen better days and was eventually towed into a cove where she was moored. Over time, the unattended vessel began to take on water and was soon on the bottom. Unfortunately, her location for divers was horrible as she was sitting in silt, and poor visibility was inevitable.

At one point in 1975, the Army Corp. of Engineers was going to blow the wreck up as they considered the ship a hazard to navigation. Around the same time, St. Thomas noticed the amount of interest their neighboring British Virgin Islands were getting since the movie "The Deep" was being

Bow of the *Cartanser Senior*. Photo courtesy Steve Simonsen.

filmed on the wreck of the *Rhone*. St. Thomas decided that they too should have a clear water wreck, and started the wheels moving to raise the *Cartanser* and move her to a spot more accessible for divers. Local divers, led by the St. Thomas Diving Club, banded together in the campaign "Save The *Cartanser*". They raised funds by selling "T" shirts stating their slogan. This effort was a huge success that will be enjoyed by divers for many years to come.

On July 16th, 1979, with the help of a giant super crane paid for by the "Save The *Cartanser*" fund, the *Cartanser Senior* was raised, moved five miles to a cove on the west side of Buck Island, and re-sunk. She is now resting in 50 feet of water, leaning on her port side. Her hull has split

Joanne Doherty on the bow section of the *Cartanser*. Photo courtesy Jeanne Tiedemann.

open and bent a little from the various storms that have passed through, but this wreck is a photographer's dream. Everything from her engine room to her bow has been photographed hundreds of times. Her remains attract not only yellow tails, tang, groupers and angelfish, but dive boats from all over the island that bring divers to explore the wreckage.

FERRY BOAT

The *Ferry Boat* is the newest wreck off the island. She was named *Mein Capitan* and used as a ferry between St. John and St. Thomas before her sinking during hurricane Gilbert. The *Ferry Boat* was raised onto a barge, but due to the extent of her damage, it was not worth repairing the vessel. The *Mein Capitan* was then taken out and dumped off the southwest end of Lovango Key. The vessel now sits upside down in 50 feet of water and has not yet fully developed as a fish haven. The *Ferry Boat* will not remain in this location for long since she was dumped without a permit. Plans are already underway to raise and relocate the wreck to a spot near the *General Rodger's* wreck. Wherever she ends up, the *Ferry Boat* should definitely become much more popular as tourists learn about her existence, and the surrounding marine life make her their new home.

GENERAL RODGER'S

The *General Rodger's* was a 120 foot long, steel hulled, auxiliary Coast Guard vessel. The ship has large reels on her stern deck which indicate that she may have once been utilized by the Coast Guard as a buoy tender. According to Steve Siminson, a local diver, she was sunk by the Coast Guard in 1972 to form an artificial reef. However, the *General Rodger's* didn't go down too easily. In fact, she took many hours before slipping beneath the ocean's surface, and during that time, she unexpectedly swung around over slightly deeper water. When the *General Rodger's* finally did sink, tragedy struck when one of the crew, who was helping to scuttle the vessel, drowned with her.

The *General Rodger's* now lies in 65 feet of water. She is not dove on as often as the *Cartanser* but is sitting upright and intact in a channel off the northwest side of St. Thomas. This wreck is fascinating to explore. Divers can swim through passageways, look out porthole openings, and can even see a huge spare propeller in her forward cargo hold. A current is usually present at this site.

The *General Rodger's* is also a great wreck to photograph. Penetration is unobstructed, and divers will find her propeller encrusted and very colorful.

Bow of the *General Rodgers*, a 120 foot long steel hulled, auxiliary Coast Guard vessel sunk in 1972. Photo by Steve Simonsen.

Looking in through one of the *General Rodgers* portholes. Photo courtesy Steve Simonsen.

The *General Rodgers* propeller is beautifully encrusted and very colorful. Photo by Steve Simonsen.

This site does not seem to attract quite as much fish life as the *Cartanser*, but large schools of small mouth grunts, barracudas, tang, and jacks can be found.

TURKS and CAICOS Eastern Caribbean

Located at the southern tip of the Bahamas are the Turks and Caicos Islands. This group of islands consists of eight large and 40 smaller islands. Grand Turk and Salt Cay, the main islands in the Turks, are separated from the Caicos by "Turks Island Passage", a deep channel 20 miles wide and over 6,000 feet deep. The Caicos' main islands are North Caicos, South Caicos, West Caicos, East Caicos, Grand Caicos and Providenciales and are all located to the northeast of the Turks. Many of the small islands and cays in this area are uninhabited, The waters around each island are pristine, warm, and clear. The area has been described as a photographer's paradise.

AIRPLANE

The *Airplane* wreck is located off South Caicos. She was a *DC-3* that had been confiscated by the government when illegal drugs were found hidden in her cargo holds.

The *Airplane* is now resting in 50 feet of water, 30 to 40 feet from the

Wing and fuselage of the *Airplane* wreck off South Caicos. Photo by Keith Ipson.

edge of a wall. Her remains are broken up and scattered, but divers will recognize her fuselage which is still intact enough to be swam through. This site is home to a wide assortment of tropical fish.

W.E. wreck in location waiting to be sunk. Photo courtesy Chloe Zimmerman.

FREIGHTER

This vessel, also known as the *W.E.* wreck, is approximately 110 feet long and weighs about 100 tons. She was sunk during the summer of 1988 by Tony Felgate and Art Pickering, local dive operators. The ship had been left rusting away on the beach for about ten years. Tony pulled her off the beach and towed her offshore where he had a few holes smashed through her hull.

As divers descend, they will reach the beginning of a canyon in 50 feet of water. By following this canyon down, divers will be lead to the *Freighter's* bow which sits in 110 feet. The ship's wheel house sits in 140 feet of water while her engine room is in 165 feet. Close by the *Freighter* wreck lies the *Southwind*.

SOUTHWIND

The *Southwind* was a 175 foot long, steel hulled island freighter. The vessel was confiscated in 1982 after authorities discovered she was being used to smuggle drugs. She was then sunk off North Provo in order to make an artificial reef.

The ships remains are very smashed up and scattered, leaving us few clues as to the shape they once held. The *Southwind* lies in 55 feet of water off the island of Provo, and is home to about 15 very tame groupers.

A diver swims toward the *Southwind's* broken bow section. Photo courtesy Tony Felgate.

The *Southwind's* stern section is still somewhat intact but most of her remains are very smashed up and scattered, leaving us few clues as to the shape they once held. Photo by Tony Felgate.

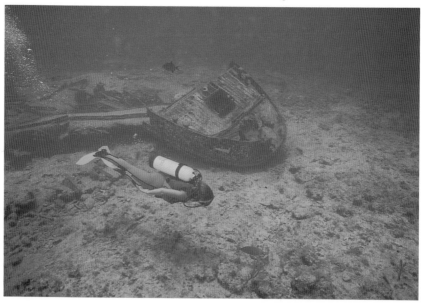

Sources of Shipwreck Information

Library of Congress
Geography and Map Division
Washington, D.C. 20540

Mariners Museum Library
Newport News, Virginia 23606

National Archives and Records Service
8th and Pennsylvania Avenues, MW
Washington, DC 20408

National Maritime Museum
Greenwich
London SE109NF

Naval Historical Center (SH)
Building 220-2
Washington Navy Yard
Washington, D.C. 20374

Peabody Museum of Salem
Phillips Library
East India Square
Salem, Mass 01970

Smithsonian Institution
Museum of American History
Washington, D.C. 20560

Steamship Historical Society of America
University of Baltimore Library
1420 Maryland Avenue
Baltimore, Md 21201

SUGGESTED READING

Berg, Daniel
>Shore Diver
>Aqua Explorers, Inc. (1987)

Berg, Daniel
>Wreck Valley
>Aqua Explorers, Inc. (1986)

Berman, Bruce
>Encyclopedia of American Shipwrecks
>Mariners Press (1972)

Blout, Steve
>The Bahamas Nassau and New Providence Island
>Pisces Books (1985)

Cohen, Shlomo
>Bahamas Diver's Guide
>Seapen Books (1977)

Davis, Bill
>Shipwrecks off the Central New Jersey Coast
>(1987)

Dethlefsen, Edwin
>Whidah
>Seafarers Heritage Library (1984)

Farb, Roderick
>Shipwrecks
>Menasha Ridge Press (1985)

Gentile, Gary
>Advanced Wreck Diving Guide
>Cornell Maritime Press (1988)

Gentile, Gary
	Andrea Doria
	Gary Gentile Productions (1989)

Gentile, Gary
	Shipwrecks Of New Jersey
	Sea Sports Publications (1988)

Haws, Duncan
	Merchant Fleets in Profile, Vol II
	(1979)

Hocking, Charles
	Dictionary of Disasters at Sea During the Age of Steam
	Lloyd's Register of Shipping (1969)

Keats, Henry. and Farr, George
	Dive into History U-Boats
	American Merchant Marine Museum Press (1986)

Keats, Henry
	New England's Legacy of Shipwrecks
	American Merchant Marine Museum Press (1988)

Kludas, Arnold
	Great Passenger Ships of the World
	Patrick Stephens

Lewbel, George
	Bonaire Curacao and Aruba
	Pisces Books (1984)

Lonsdale, Adrain L. and Kaplan, H.R.
	A Guide to Sunken Ships in American Waters
	Compass Publications, (1964)

Mathewson, Duncan
      Treasure of the Atocha
      Pisces Books (1986)

Marler, George and Luana
      The Royal Mail Steamer Rhone
      Marler Publications Ltd (1978)

Marx, Robert
      Shipwrecks in the Americas
      Bonanza Books (1983)

Metery, Michel
      Tamaya
      (1984)

Overshiner, Elwyn
      Course 095 to Eternity
      Elwyn E. Overshiner (1980)

Peterson, Mendal
      History Under the Sea
      Mendel Peterson (1973)

Quinn, William
      Shipwrecks around New England
      The Lower Cape Publishing Co. (1979)

Smith, Eugene
      Passenger Ships of the World Past and Present
      George H. Dean Company (1978)

DIVE SHOP DIRECTORY

BAHAMAS

ABACO

ABACO DIVING
VACATIONS
101 F St
St Augustine Beach, Fl
32084
(904) 471-5558

BRENDALS DIVE
SHOP
Green Turtle Cay
Abaco, Bahamas
(809) 367-2572
(800) 468-9876

DIVE ABACO
Box 555 Marsh Harbor
Abaco, Bahamas
(809) 367-2787
(800) 468-9876

ISLAND MARINE
DIVE SHOP
Box G Hope Town
Abaco, Bahamas
(809) 367-2822

WALKERS CAY
DIVERS
700 S.W. 34 St

Ft. Lauderdale FL
33315
(305) 522-1469
(800) 327-3714

ANDROS

NEAL WATSON'S
UNDERSEA
ADVENTURES
Box 21766
Fort Lauderdale, Fl.
33335
(305) 763-2188
(800) 327-8150

SMALL HOPE BAY
LODGE DIVING
Box 21667
Fort Lauderdale, Fl.
33335
(305) 463-9130
(809) 368-2014
(800) 223-6961

BERRY ISLANDS

CHUB CAY CLUB
Box 661067
Miami Springs, Fl.
33266
(305) 445-7830
(809) 325-1490

NEAL WATSON'S
UNDERSEA

ADVENTURES
Box 21766
Fort Lauderdale, Fl.
33335
(305) 763-2188
(800) 327-8150

BIMINI

BILL AND NOWDLAS
BIMINI UNDERSEA
ADVENTURE
Box 21766
Fort Lauderdale, Fl.
33335
(305) 763-2188
(800) 327-8150

ELEUTHERA

COTTON BAY CLUB
Box 28
Rock Sound, Eleuthera,
Bahamas
(212) 661-4540
(809) 334-6101
(800) 223-1588

ROMORA BAY DIVE
CLUB
Box 7206
Boca Raton, Fl. 33431
(305) 760-4535
(809) 333-2325
(800) 327-8286

SPANISH WELLS
DIVE CENTER
Box 31
Spanish Wells,

Eleuthera, Bahamas
(305) 341-9173
(800) 262-0621

VALENTINE'S DIVE
CENTER
3928 Shelbyville Road
Louisville, Kentucky
40207
(502) 897-6481
(809) 333-2309

GRAND BAHAMA

DEEP WATER CAY
CLUB
P.O. Box 1145
Palm Beach, FL 33480
(407) 684-3958

UNEXSO
1628 S.E. 10th Terrace,
Room 203
Fort Lauderdale, Fl.
33316
(305) 761-7679
(809) 373-1244
(800) 992-3483

WEST END DIVING
CENTER
Box 2433, Freeport
Grand Bahama,
Bahamas
(305) 761-7679
(809) 346-6211
(800) 992-3483

LONG ISLAND

STELLA MARIS INN
DIVING
701 S.W. 48th Street
Fort Lauderdale, FL
33315
(305) 467-0466
(809) 336-2106
(800) 426-0466

NEW PROVIDENCE

Bahama Divers Ltd
P.O. Box SS-5004
Nassau, Bahamas
(809) 326-5644
(809) 322-8431

DIVE   DIVE   DIVE
LTD.
Box N
Nassau, Bahamas
(809) 326-1143
(800) 328-8029

STUART COVE'S
NASSAU UNDERSEA
ADVENTURES
Box CB 11697
Nassau, Bahamas
(809) 327-7862
(800) 468-9876

PETER HUGHES
DIVE SOUTH OCEAN
54 Gunderman RD
Ithaca, N.Y. 14850
(607) 277-3484
(800) 367-3484

SUN DIVERS
Box N 10728
Nassau, Bahamas
(809) 325-8927

SUN SKIFF DIVERS
Ltd
P.O. Box N-142
Nassau, Bahamas
(809) 328-4075
(800) 548-8570

RUM CAY

RUM CAY CLUB
DIVING
Box 22396
Fort Lauderdale, FL
33335
(305) 467-8355
(809) 332-2103
(800) 334-6869

SAN SALVADOR

GUANAHANI DIVE
LTD
701 S.W. 48th Street
Fort Lauderdale, FL
33315
(305) 761-1492
(800) 272-1492

RUM CAY CLUB
Po Box 22396
Ft   Lauderdale,   FL
33335
(305) 467-8355
(800) 334-6869

CARIBBEAN

ANTIGUA

DIVE ANTIGUA
Box 251
St. John's, Antigua
(809) 462-0256

DIVE RUNAWAY
Box 1370
St. John's, Antigua
(809) 462-2626

JOLLY DIVE
Box 744
St. John's, Antigua
(809) 462-0061
(800) 321-1055

ARUBA

PELICAN
WATERSPORTS
Box 36 Oranjestad
Aruba
(001) 297-823888

SCUBA ARUBA
PO Box 294
San Nicolaas, Aruba
(011) 297-834142

BARBADOS

DIVE BOAT SAFARI
Needhas Point

Barbados
(809) 429-8216

JOLLY ROGER
WATERSPORTS
Bridgetown Harbour
Bridgetown, Barbados
(703) 893-4704
(809) 432-7090

PETER HUGHES
UNDERWATER
BARBADOS
3504 St. Lawrence Gap
Church
Barbados
(607) 277-3484
(809) 428-3504
(800) 367-3484

SCOTCH & SODA
DIVERS
St. Lawrence Gap
Christ Church
Barbados
(809) 428-7308

THE DIVE SHOP
LTD.
PO Box 44-B
Saint Michael, Barbados
(809) 426-9947
(809) 426-2031

WILLIE'S
WATERSPORTS
Black Rock
Saint   Michaels   ,

Barbados
(809) 425-1060
(809) 424-1808

BELIZE

CORAL BEACH DIVE
CLUB
San Pedro
Ambergris Caye, Belize
(800) 348-9101

DIVE BELIZE
Box 625
Belize City, Belize
(714) 955-2774
(800) 854-9303
(011) 501-44190

BONAIRE

BONAIRE   SCUBA
CENTER
Box 755
Morgan N.J. 08879
(201) 566-8866
(011) 599-78978
(800) 526-3270

BRUCE   BOWKERS
CARIB INN
PO Box 68
Bonaire, N.A.
(011) 599-78819

BUDDY'S DIVE
RESORT
1200 Box 231
Bonaire, N.A.

(212) 662-4858
(011) 599-78647

CAPTAIN DON'S
HABITAT
Box 88
Bonaire, N.A.
(802) 492-5607
(800) 345-0322

DIVE INN
Helmut Rd
Bonaire, N.A.
(011) 599-78761

PETER HUGHES
DIVE BONAIRE
54 Gunderman Rd
Ithaca, N.Y. 14850
(607) 277-3484
(800) 367-3484
(011) 599-78285

SAND DOLLAR DIVE
AND PHOTO
50 Georgetown Rd
Bordentown NJ 08505
(609) 298-2298
(011) 599-78738

TOUCH THE SEA
WITH DEE SCARR
PO Box 369
Bonaire, N.A.
(011) 599-78529

BRITISH   VIRGIN ISLANDS

BASKIN IN THE SUN
PO Box 108
Tortola, B.V.I.
(800) 233-7938
(809) 494-2858

BLUE WATER
DIVERS
Box 437
Roadtown   Tortola,
B.V.I.
(809) 494-2847

DIVE BVI
Box 1040 Virgin Gorda
Yacht Virgin Gorda,
B.V.I.
(809) 495-5513

ISLAND DIVER LTD
Box 3023
Road Town Tortola,
B.V.I.
(809) 494-3878

KILBRIDE U/W
TOURS
Box 40
Virgin Gorda, B.V.I.
(809) 496-0111

RAINBOW VISIONS
PHOTOGRAPHY
PO Box 108
Roadtown,   Tortola,
B.V.I.
(809) 44-2749

TROPIC BIRD

(800) 433-DIVE
(805) 654-8100

UNDERWATER
SAFARIS
PO Box 139
Road Town, Tortola,
B.V.I.
(809) 494-3235
(800) 535-7289

CAYMAN BRAC

BRAC AQUATICS
LTD
Box 89 West End
Cayman Brac, Cayman
Islands
(809) 948-7429

PETER HUGHES
DIVE TIARA
54 Gunderman Rd
Ithaca, N.Y. 14850
(607) 277-3484
(809) 948-7313
(800) 367-3484

COZUMEL

DISCOVER
COZUMEL
Po Box 75
Cozumel, Q   Roo,
Mexico 77600
(987) 2-02-80
(800) 32805285

DIVE PARADISE
170 Denny Way

Seattle, WA 8109
(206) 441-3483
(800) 247-3483

FANTASIA DIVERS
(713) 558-9524
(800) 336-3483

MICHELLE'S DIVE
SHOP
PO Box 75
Cozumel, Q Roo,
Mexico 77600
(987) 2-09-47

SCUBA COZUMEL
Po Box 289
Cozumel, Q Roo,
Mexico 77600
(800) 847-5708

CURACAO

CORAL CLIFF
DIVING
Box 3782
Curacao, N.A.
(800) 782-5247

DIVE CURACAO
Martin Luther King
Blvd
Curacao, N.A.
(212) 840-6636
(800) 223-9815

LAS PALMAS REEF
DIVERS
Box 2179
Curacao, N.A.

(203) 849-1470
(800) 622-7836

MASTER DIVE SHOP
Box 3582, Santa Martha
Curacao, N.A.
(011) 599-9611772

SEASCAPE
Curacao Caribbean
Hotel
Box 2133
Curacao, N.A.
(212) 697-7746
(800) 422-0866
(011) 599-9625000

UNDERWATER
CURACAO
Seaquarium
Curacau, N.A.
(800) 782-5247

GRAND CAYMAN

BOB SOTO'S DIVING
Box 1801
Grand Cayman, Cayman
Islands
(809) 949-2022
(800) 262-7686

CAYMAN DIVING
LODGE
Box 1308
Grand Cayman, Cayman
Islands
(809) 949-4729

CAYMAN KAI

RESORTS
Box 1112
Grand   Cayman   ,
Cayman Islands
(305) 554-9350
(809) 947-9055
(800) 223-5427

DIVER'S WORLD
Box 917
Grand Cayman, Cayman
Islands
(809) 949-8128

DON FOSTER'S
Box 151
Grand Cayman, Cayman
Islands
(809) 949-7025
(809) 949-5679

EDEN ROCK DIVING
CENTER
Box 1907
Grand Cayman, Cayman
Islands
(809) 949-7243

FISHEYE
PHOTOGRAPHY
Box 2123
Grand Cayman, Cayman
Islands
(809) 947-4209

NICK'S AQUA
SPORTS
10   South   Riverside
Plaza
Suite 2

Chicago, IL. 60606

RESEARCH
SUBMERSIBLES
LIMITED
Box 1719
Grand Cayman, Cayman
Islands
(809) 949-8296
(809) 949-7421

RIVERS SPORT
DIVERS
Box 442 West Bay
Grand Cayman, Cayman
Islands
(809) 949-1181

SEA SPORTS
Box 431 West Bay
Grand Cayman, Cayman
Islands
(809) 949-3965
(800) 949-3965

SPANISH COVE
Box 637
Grand Cayman, Cayman
Islands
(809) 949-3675
(800) 231-4610

SUNSET DIVERS
Box 479
Grand   Cayman   ,
Cayman Islands
(809) 949-7111
(800) 949-7111

SURFSIDE

WATERSPORTS
Box 891
Georgetown
Grand Cayman, Cayman
Islands
(809) 947-4244
(800) 468-1708

TORTUGA CLUB
Box 496
Georgetown
Grand Cayman, Cayman
Islands
(809) 947-7511
(800) 327-8223

TREASURE ISLAND
DIVERS
Box 1817
Georgetown
Grand Cayman, Cayman
Islands
(809) 949-7777
(800) 874-0027

GRENADA

H.M.C. DIVE
CENTER
c/o Coyaba Hotel
Grand Anse Beach
St. George's Grenada.
W.I.
(809) 444-4129

HORSE SHOE
BEACH HOTEL
Box 174
St. Georges, Grenada

W.I.
(809) 444-4010
(809) 444-4244

UNDERWATER
DISCOVERY   of
GRENADA
c/o 27222
Route 37 East
Toms River, N.J. 08753
(201) 270-9100

VIRGO
WATERSPORTS
Box 174
St. Georges, Grenada
W.I.
(809) 444-4410

GUANAJA

BAYMAN BAY CLUB
Guanaja
Bay Islands, Honduras,
CCA
(800) 524-1823

POSADA DEL SOL
PO Box 537
Boca Raton, Fl. 33429
(305) 944-8544
(800) 642-3483

JAMAICA

CLUB CARRIBEAN
SUN DIVERS
PO Box 65 Runaway
Bay

Jamaica, W.I.
(809) 973-3507
(800) 223-6510

FANTASEA DIVERS
Box 103
Ocho Rios, Jamaica
(809) 974-5344

HONEY'S WATERSPORTS
(809) 957-4467
(809) 957-4408

NEGRIL SCUBA
CENTER
Negril Beach Club
Negril, Jamaica, W.I.
(809) 957-4425

POSEIDON NEMROD
DIVERS
Box 152 Reading
St. James, Jamaica
(809) 952-3624

SUN DIVERS
PO Box 212
Runaway Bay, Jamaica,
W.I.
(809) 973-2346

LITTLE CAYMAN

SAM MCCOY'S
DIVING LODGE
14 Rochambeau Avenue
Ridgefield, CT. 06877
(203) 438-5663
(809) 948-8326

SOUTHERN CROSS
CLUB
1005 East Towen #1
Merchant Plaza
Indanapolis, IN. 46204
(317) 636-9501
(809) 948-3255

MARTINIQUE

BATHY'S CLUB
HOTEL MERIDAN
La Poin du Bount
97229 Trois llets
Martinique, F.W.I.
(011) 596-660000

HELICARAIBES
40, rue Ernest Deproge
Fort de France
Martinique, F.W.I.
(011) 596-733003

SUB DIAMOND
ROCK
Novotel Diamant
Point de la Chery
97223   Diamant
Martinique, F.W.I.
(011) 596-764242

TROPICASUB
DIVING CENTER
C/O Hotel La Bateliere
97233 Schoelcher
Martinique, F.W.I.
(011) 596-614949

PUERTO RICO

CARIBBEAN
MARINE SERVICES
Box 467
Culebra PR 00645
(809) 742-3555

CARIBBEAN
SCHOOL OF
AQUATICS
Box 4195
San Jaun PR 00905
(809) 728-6606

CARIBE AQUATIC
ADVENTURES
Box 1872
San Jaun PR 00903
(809) 721-0303

CORAL HEAD
DIVERS
Box CUHF
Humacao PR 00601
(809) 850-7208
(800) 221-4874

DORADO MARINE
CENTER
PO Box 705
Dorado, PR 00646
(809) 796-4645

LA CUEVA
SUBMARINA
Box 151 Isabela PR
00662
(809) 872-3903

MARINE SPORTS &
DIVE
Perla Del Sur Z-507
Box 7711
Ponce PR 00732
(809) 844-6175

MUNDO
SUBMARINO
Laguna Gardens
Shopping Center
Isla Verde PR 00913

PARGUERADIVERS
Box 514
Lajas PR 00667
(809) 899-4171

SCUBA CENTRO
1156 Roosevelt Avenue
Puerto Nuevo, PR
00920
(809) 781-8086

SCUBA SHOP
Villa Marina Shopping
Center #6
Fajardo PR 00648
(809) 863-8465

ROATAN

ANTHONY'S KEY
RESORT
1385 Coral Way, Suite
401
Maimi FL 33145
(305) 858-3483
(800) 227-3483

COCO VIEW RESORT
Box 877
San Antonio FL 33576
(904) 588-4131
(800) 282-8932

ST. CROIX

CARRIBEAN SEA &
REEF CHARTERS
Box 3881 Christiansted
St. Croix V.I. 00820
(809) 773-5922

DIVE EXPERIENCE
Box 4254
Christansted, St. Croix
VI 00820
(809) 773-3307

SEA SHADOWS
SCUBA
Po Box 505
Cane Bay, St. Croix VI
00820
(809) 778-3850

V.I. DIVERS LIMITED
Panam Pavilion
St. Croix, V.I. 00820
(809) 773-6045

ST. EUSTATIUS

DIVE STATIA
Box 172
St. Eustatius, N.A.
(800) 468-1708
(011) 599-32319

ST. KITTS

KENNETH'S DIVE
CENTER
Newtown Bay Road
Bassetere, St. Kitts
(809) 465-2670

NEVIS WATER
SPORTS
Quali Beach Nevis
(809) 469-9518

ST. LUCIA

SCUBA ST. LUCIA
Anse Chastanet Hotel
Box 216
Soufriere, St. Lucia
(809) 454-7354

ST. MAARTEN

MAHO
WATERSPORTS
Box 520368
Miami, Fl. 33152
(011) 599-544387

OCEAN EXPLORERS
Simpson Bay St.
St. Maarten, N.A.
(011) 599-545252
(011) 599-542220

SEA DANCER
54 Gunderman Road

Ithaca, NY 14850
(800) 367-3484
(607) 277-3484

TRADE WINDS DIVE
CENTER
Great Bay Marina
Philpsburg, St. Maarten
N.A.

ST. VINCENT & THE GRENADINES

DIVE BEQUIA
Box 16
St. Vincent
(809) 458-3425

DIVE MUSTIQUE
Box 16
St. Vincent
(809) 458-3504

DIVE ST. VINCENT
LTD.
Box 864
St. Vincent
(809) 457-4714
(809) 457-4409

ST. THOMAS

AQUA ACTION
WATER SPORTS
Box 12138
St. Thomas, V.I. 00801
(809) 775-6285

SEA ADVENTURES

Box 9531
St. Thomas, V.I. 00801
(809) 774-9652
(800) 524-2096

TURKS AND CAICOS

PROVO   AQUATIC
CENTER
Providenciales
Turks & Caicos Islands
(809) 946-4455
(800) 351-8261

PROVO   TURTLE
DIVERS
Box 52-6002
Miami, Fl. 33152
(809) 946-4232
(800) 328-5285

PROVO UNDERSEA
ADVENTURES
Turtle Cove Yacht and
Tennis Resort
Providenciales

Turks & Caicos Islands
(305) 763-2188
(809) 946-2043
(800) 237-8150

SEA TOPIA
Box 52-6002 #16
Miami, Fl. 33152
(305) 665-0198
(809) 946-4553

THIRD TURTLE

DIVERS
Providenciales
Turks & Caicos Islands
(809) 946-4230
(800) 323-7600

Aqua Explorers Inc. does not recommend any particular dive operator, or the qualifications and competence of any of the above listed operators. This directory was assembled for the convenience of our readers and is not a complete list of all dive facilities through out the Bahamas and Caribbean. If a scuba related shop or operation would like to be listed at our next printing please contact the publisher.

INDEX

Other Products Available
From
Aqua Explorers Inc

WRECK VALLEY

The history and legend of 58 shipwrecks all located just of Long Island N.Y.'s South Shore, are explored in the book, *Wreck Valley*, by Daniel Berg.

Dan has combed many of the ships himself. He's combined his own discoveries with extensive research and illustrated the 84 page softcover book with six maps, 51 modern and historic photographs and 14 drawings of the wrecks as they rest now on the ocean floor. Copies available for $ 12.95

LORAN "C" LIST

Wreck Valleys shipwreck locations finally disclosed! Our *Loran "C" List*, by Daniel Berg and Steve Bielenda, was designed to be a weather proof tool for fishermen and divers alike. On this list you will find not only over sixty accurate loran numbers, but also wrecks depth and reference page number where historical information can be found in the book *Wreck Valley*. Available for $ 14.95

SHORE DIVER

Over forty Long Island N.Y. beach dive locations are described and explored in detail in this book titled *Shore Diver*, by Daniel Berg.

This illustrated 96 page softcover book contains a topside photograph of each location, two historic ship photographs, fifteen under water photographs, eight maps plus pertinent information such as easy to follow street directions, depth of water, bottom composition, currents and overall dive conditions. Copies available for $ 12.95

GRAND CAYMAN SHIPWRECK VIDEO

Aqua Explorers, Inc., recently completed a documentary, filmed by veteran wreck divers, author Daniel Berg and Steve Bielenda, on the shipwrecks of Grand Cayman. This one hour video serves as a vacationing sport diver's guide to diving Cayman's shipwrecks. Historical information on each wreck is included as well as topside shots and underwater footage of the Gamma, Callie, Balboa, Oro Verde, Carrie Lee, and Kirk Pride.

Also captured on video: a diver petting a 300 pound grouper; catching a 8 pound rock lobster; and penetrating deep inside the Ore Verde. A two-man submersible allowed film makers to record the 800 foot deep wreck of the Kirk Pride. Available for $ 41.95.

Aqua Explorers Inc.
P.O. Box 116
East Rockaway N.Y. 11510